*Guide to the Great Florida Birding Trail*

Florida A&M University, Tallahassee
Florida Atlantic University, Boca Raton
Florida Gulf Coast University, Ft. Myers
Florida International University, Miami
Florida State University, Tallahassee
University of Central Florida, Orlando
University of Florida, Gainesville
University of North Florida, Jacksonville
University of South Florida, Tampa
University of West Florida, Pensacola

A project of the Florida Fish and Wildlife
Conservation Commission

University Press of Florida
Gainesville · Tallahassee · Tampa · Boca Raton
Pensacola · Orlando · Miami · Jacksonville · Ft. Myers

GUIDE TO THE

Great
Florida
Birding
Trail

EAST SECTION

Edited by Julie A. Brashears and Susan I. Cerulean

Illustrations by Nancy Meyer

Copyright 2002 by the Wildlife Foundation of Florida, Inc.
Printed in Canada on acid-free paper

07 06 05 04 03 02   6 5 4 3 2 1

Library of Congress Cataloging-in-Publication Data
Guide to the Great Florida Birding Trail. East Section: a project
of the Florida Fish and Wildlife Conservation Commission /
edited by Julie A. Brashears and Susan I. Cerulean.
p. cm.
Includes bibliographical references.
ISBN 0-8130-2561-3 (paper: alk. paper)
1. Bird watching—Florida—Guidebooks. 2. Florida—Guidebooks.
I. Brashears, Julie A. II. Cerulean, Susan. III. Florida Fish & Wildlife
Conservation Commission.
QL684.F6 G85 2002
598'.07'234759—dc21   2002072731

The University Press of Florida is the scholarly publishing agency
for the State University System of Florida, comprising Florida A&M
University, Florida Atlantic University, Florida Gulf Coast University,
Florida International University, Florida State University, University
of Central Florida, University of Florida, University of North Florida,
University of South Florida, and University of West Florida.

University Press of Florida
15 Northwest 15th Street
Gainesville, FL 32611-2079
http://www.upf.com

Contents

List of Maps xi

Preface xiii

How to Use This Guide xv

Birding Ethics xvii
  Ann Morrow

Essay: Gateway to the Great Florida Birding Trail: Fort Clinch State Park 1
  Ann Morrow

Gannet Cluster 4

  1. Fort Clinch State Park 5
  2. The Nature Center at Amelia Island Plantation 5
  3. Amelia Island State Park 6
  4. Big Talbot Island State Park 7
  5. Little Talbot Island State Park 7
  6. E. Dale Joyner Nature Preserve at Pelotes Island 8
  7. Cedar Point 9
  8. Kingsley Plantation 9
  9. Fort George Island Cultural State Park 10
  10. Huguenot Memorial Park 11
  11. Fort Caroline National Memorial and Theodore Roosevelt Area 12
  12. Kathryn Abbey Hanna Park 13

Essay: Painted Buntings in Florida: The End of the Rainbow Holds No Gold 14
  Jim Cox

Essay: Birds at Sea, Birders on the Coast 17
  Noel Wamer

St. Marys Cluster 19

  13. Ralph E. Simmons State Forest 20

Kestrel Cluster 21

  14. Jennings State Forest 22
  15. Mike Roess Gold Head Branch State Park 23

Essay: Fall Migration of Raptors: Why, When, and Where 24
  Matthew Mullenix

Painted Bunting Cluster   26

16. Guana River Wildlife Management Area   27
17. Guana River State Park   27
18. St. Augustine Alligator Farm   28
19. Anastasia State Park   29
20. Fort Matanzas National Monument   29
21. Faver-Dykes State Park   30
22. Princess Place Preserve   31
23. Washington Oaks Gardens State Park   32

Essay: Birdwatching 101: Identification Basics   33
   Jim Cox

Upland Songbird Cluster   37

24. Ravine Gardens State Park   38
25. Caravelle Ranch Wildlife Management Area   38
26. Welaka State Forest   39
27. Welaka National Fish Hatchery and Aquarium   40
28. Ocala National Forest: Salt Springs   41

Essay: The Unexpected Economics of Birding   42
   Julie A. Brashears

Limpkin Cluster   46

29. Sportsman's Cove   47
30. Silver River State Park   47
31. Ocklawaha Prairie Restoration Area   48

Essay: Florida's Fabulous Waders   49
   Susan D. Jewell

Warbler Hammocks Cluster   51

32. Haw Creek Preserve at Russell Landing   52
33. Bulow Creek State Park   52
34. North Peninsula State Park   53
35. Tomoka State Park   54

Essay: Swallow-Tailed Kites: Masters of the Wind   55
   Ken Meyer

Swallow-Tailed Kite Cluster   57

36. Ocala National Forest: Alexander Springs   58
37. Sunnyhill Restoration Area   58
38. Emeralda Marsh Conservation Area   59
39. Emeralda Marsh Conservation Area (Treasure Island Entrance)   59
40. Hidden Waters Preserve   60

Essay: Bird Migration: A Biannual Stretching of the Wings   61
    Jim Cox

Essay: The Scrub and the Scrub-Jay: Imperiled Natural Treasures of Florida   63
    Reed Bowman and Glen Woolfenden

Scrub-Jay Cluster   65

41. Lake George State Forest   66
42. DeLeon Springs State Park   66
43. Lake Woodruff National Wildlife Refuge   67
44. Hontoon Island State Park   68
45. Blue Spring State Park   68
46. Lyonia Preserve   69
47. Lake Ashby Park   70
48. Smyrna Dunes Park   71

Essay: Birdwatching 101: The Tools of the Trade   72
    Jim Cox

Tanager Cluster   76

49. Rock Springs Run State Reserve   77
50. Seminole State Forest   77
51. Lower Wekiva River Preserve State Park   78
52. Wekiwa Springs State Park   79
53. Lake Jesup Wilderness Area   79
54. Audubon Center for Birds of Prey   80
55. Mead Gardens   81

Essay: A Beach in the Sky   82
    Jeff Gore

Bittern and Bobwhite Cluster   84

56. Lake Proctor Wilderness Area   85
57. Geneva Wilderness Area   85
58. Little Big Econ State Forest: Kilbee Tract   86
59. Little Big Econ State Forest: Demetree Tract   86
60. Orlando Wetlands Park   87
61. Tosohatchee State Reserve   88

Essay: Gateway to the Great Florida Birding Trail: Merritt Island National Wildlife
    Refuge   89
    Joanna Taylor

River to Ocean Cluster   92

62. Merritt Island National Wildlife Refuge   93
63. Canaveral National Seashore (North Entrance)   93
64. River Breeze Park   94

65. Scottsmoor Landing 95

66. Buck Lake Conservation Area (West Entrance) 95

67. Buck Lake Conservation Area (East Entrance) 95

68. Seminole Ranch Conservation Area 96

69. Parrish Park–Titusville 97

70. Canaveral National Seashore (South Entrance) 97

71. Hatbill Park 98

Essay: Demise of the Dusky 99
   Jim Cox

Natural Attractions Cluster 101

72. Lake Louisa State Park 102

73. Tibet-Butler Preserve 102

74. Gatorland 103

75. The Nature Conservancy's Disney Wilderness Preserve 104

Essay: Burning for Birds: Why Birders Should Support the Use of Prescribed Fire 105
   R. Todd Engstrom

Turkey Cluster 107

76. Moss Park 108

77. Split Oak Mitigation Park 108

78. Lake Lizzie Nature Preserve 109

Essay: Birdwatching 101: Birding by Ear 110
   Jim Cox

Teal Cluster 113

79. Fox Lake Park 114

80. Blue Heron Wetlands Treatment Facility 114

81. Kennedy Point Park 115

82. Pine Island Conservation Area 116

83. J. G. Bourbeau Park 116

84. Kelly Park 117

85. Port's End Park 117

86. Jetty Maritime Park 118

87. Rotary Park at Merritt Island 119

88. Lori Wilson Park 119

Essay: When Birds Can't Rise Above the Fray 120
   Jim Cox

Essay: Gateway to the Great Florida Birding Trail:
   Tenoroc Fish Management Area 122
   Jenny Novak

Purple Gallinule Cluster   124

89. Tenoroc Fish Management Area   125
90. Saddle Creek Park   126
91. Lake Hollingsworth   126
92. Peace River Park   127

Essay: Birding the Lake Wales Ridge   128
     Tom Palmer

Ridge Cluster   130

93. Lake Region Audubon's Street Nature Center   131
94. Eagle Ridge Mall   131
95. Lake Kissimmee State Park   132
96. Bok Tower Gardens   132
97. Lake Wailes   133
98. Ridge Audubon Nature Center   134
99. Lake Wales Ridge State Forest: Walk-in-the-Water Tract   134
100. Lake Wales Ridge State Forest: Arbuckle Tract   135

Essay: Whooping Cranes Return to Florida   136
     Steve Nesbitt

Whooping Crane Cluster   138

101. Forever Florida   139
102. Joe Overstreet Landing   139
103. Three Lakes Wildlife Management Area   140

Essay: A Vote for the Land   141
     Ann Morrow

Migrant Fallout Cluster   143

104. Brevard Zoo   144
105. Rotary Park at Suntree   144
106. Wickham Park   145
107. Lake Washington Park   145
108. Lake Washington: Sarno Road Extension   145
109. Erna Nixon Park   146
110. Turkey Creek Sanctuary   146
111. Malabar Scrub Sanctuary   147
112. Coconut Point Park   147
113. Honest John's Fish Camp   148

Essay: Made in the Shade   149
     Ann Morrow
Essay: It's a Matter of Survival: Shorebirds on the Beach   151
     Nancy Douglass

Vero Vireo Cluster   153

114. T. M. Goodwin Waterfowl Management Area   154
115. St. Sebastian River State Buffer Preserve (North Entrance)   154
116. St. Sebastian River State Buffer Preserve (South Entrance)   154
117. Sebastian Inlet State Park   155
118. Environmental Learning Center   156
119. Blue Cypress Conservation Area   157
120. Indian River County Wetlands Treatment Facility   157
121. Oslo Riverfront Conservation Area (ORCA)   158

Essay: Crested Caracara: Florida Prairie Specialty   159
    Joan Morrison

Scrub and Stream Cluster   161

122. Highlands Hammock State Park   162
123. Istokpoga Park   162
124. Hickory Hammock   163
125. Lake June-in-Winter Scrub State Park   164

Essay: Ode to a Sparrow   165
    Paul Gray

Caracara Cluster   167

126. Prairie Bird Long Loop (Starting Point)   168
127. Prairie Bird Short Loop (Starting Point)   168
128. Kissimmee Prairie Preserve State Park   168
129. Lock 7: Jaycee Park   169
130. Okee-Tantie   170

Essay: Un-straightening the Kissimmee River   171
    Paul Gray

Sandhill Crane Cluster   173

131. Indrio Savannahs   174
132. Fort Pierce Inlet State Park   174
133. Bear Point Sanctuary   175
134. Pinelands   175
135. Savannas Preserve State Park   176

Resources for Birdwatchers   177

Index Chart   181
List of Contributors   187

Maps

Full section map with numbered locator squares   xix

First subsection map: top third (Nassau, Duval, Clay, St. Johns, and Putnam Counties)   3

1. Gannet Cluster   4
2. St. Marys Cluster   19
3. Kestrel Cluster   21
4. Painted Bunting Cluster   26
5. Upland Songbird Cluster   37

Second subsection map: middle third (Flagler, Marion, Lake, Volusia, Seminole, and Orange Counties)   45

6. Limpkin Cluster   46
7. Warbler Hammocks Cluster   51
8. Swallow-Tailed Kite Cluster   57
9. Scrub-Jay Cluster   65
10. Tanager Cluster   76
11. Bittern and Bobwhite Cluster   84

Third subsection map: bottom third (Brevard, Polk, Osceola, Indian River, Highlands, Okeechobee, and St. Lucie Counties)   91

12. River to Ocean Cluster   92
13. Natural Attractions Cluster   101
14. Turkey Cluster   107
15. Teal Cluster   113
16. Purple Gallinule Cluster   124
17. Ridge Cluster   130
18. Whooping Crane Cluster   138
19. Migrant Fallout Cluster   143
20. Vero Vireo Cluster   153
21. Scrub and Stream Cluster   161
22. Caracara Cluster   167
23. Sandhill Crane Cluster   173

Preface

Guide to the Great Florida Birding Trail is a new kind of birding guide—one that makes it easy for you to view birds today while working to conserve birds for tomorrow. In a state where tourists more often see animated wildlife than real, our lifestyles tend to keep nature at bay with air-conditioning, pavement, and glass. However, the tide is turning. In 1996 Florida was second only to California in the number of people participating in wildlife viewing. In a 1998 study, nearly half of American households surveyed said they enjoyed a nature-based activity on their last vacation. Outdoor recreation is soaring, and birdwatching is the fastest-growing outdoor hobby in the nation.[1]

In hopes of encouraging this trend, the Florida Fish and Wildlife Conservation Commission, through its Watchable Wildlife Program, created the Great Florida Birding Trail. The Trail is based on a collection of sites throughout Florida identified for their excellent birdwatching or bird education opportunities. We hope the Trail will help you to enjoy and appreciate Florida's wild bird life, and to support conservation of these birds and their habitats.

Traditionally, conservation has been at odds with economic development. Development brought prosperity, but once those communities were prosperous and took a moment to look around, many regretted the nature they had lost. The Birding Trail is part of a trend, to use tourist dollars to motivate the conservation of our wildlands. By giving our natural areas economic value in the form of tourism dollars, we can make wildland conservation an economic alternative for landowners. We also hope the Trail will motivate more developed areas to shepherd their remaining resources, and restore some of what they may have already cleared.

The first section of the Trail—East Florida—is the bold beginning of this statewide initiative. It identifies sites by geographic location and types of bird you're likely to see. Additionally, it informs you about the seasonality of those species, how long your visit to each site could last, and what educational opportunities are available. So flip through the guide and find a spot to go birding near you! Who ever thought conservation could be so much fun?

Many thanks to the Florida Department of Transportation for their generous funding of the East Florida Birding Trail, and to the Florida Fish and Wildlife Conservation Commission, for conceiving and hosting the project. The birders and citizen conservationists, tourism professionals and government officials who nominated sites are the reason this program exists, and the land managers who assisted with site visits and descriptions were valued collaborators. Their dedication and vision are humbling and inspiring. The steering committee's patience and wisdom shaped this project throughout.

The essays by Paul Gray and Steve Nesbitt are included with the permission of Audubon of Florida.

Notes

1. H. Ken Cordell and Nancy G. Herbert, "The Popularity of Birding Is Growing," *Birding* (Feb. 2002).

How to Use This Guide

Whether you're a veteran birder or a beginner, this guide has been designed to help you identify quickly and easily the birding sites of interest to you. The Birding Trail's name is a bit of a misnomer, because it is not a linear arrangement of birding sites. Instead it is a collection of sites that, having met a series of criteria, are found to be good for birdwatching but not too sensitive to withstand large-scale birder use.

Organization

Sites have been arranged in "clusters," or groups of up to a dozen sites, all within an hour's drive of one another, each with its own map. Directions to sites are from the nearest large intersection. We've also included regional maps so you can easily see the density of sites in the area you're visiting. You may want to use the maps in this guide along with a larger map book, such as a DeLorme *Florida Atlas & Gazetteer*, to help you find those back roads between sites that are so good for roadside birding. Descriptions of sites follow the map for each cluster, and icons accompany each site. Begin with a region, a single location, or a single species you'd like to explore; this book should help you minimize your planning time and maximize your birding.

Planning a Trip

Most of these sites are best experienced in the company of sunscreen, bug spray, and drinking water. Plan accordingly before your trip, and call ahead for reservations for sites that are listed "by appointment only." Many sites are most productive, birdwise, at certain times of year because of migrations or nesting seasons; be sure to check the seasonality of a site before spending your time traveling there.

Gateways

If you have further questions, three great resources are available: the Trail's gateways at Fort Clinch State Park (Nassau County), Merritt Island National Wildlife Refuge (Brevard County), and Tenoroc Fish Management Area (Polk County).

These sites have staff on hand to answer questions about the Trail, kiosks with information about the Trail's structure, and visitor centers which offer information about birding classes and events occurring across the state.

How Did We Do?

Have further questions or comments about the Trail? Let us know what you think! E-mail us directly through the Trail's website, www.floridabirdingtrail.com.

Happy trails and happy birding!

Birding Ethics

Ann Morrow

Don't you hate it when the doorbell or telephone rings just as you settle down to dinner or a nap? While mere nuisances to us, disruptions in feeding and resting routines can spell disaster for birds, especially the cumulative effect of frequent disruptions, a common occurrence on busy beaches or waterways. When a nesting bird is forced to fly, it may leave eggs or young exposed to temperature extremes or predators. A migratory bird may be exhausted and hungry from a long flight—it needs to rest and eat. With care and common sense, birders can help protect the birds they love to watch.

The best birdwatchers are the quietest and least intrusive.

- Stay back from concentrations of nesting or loafing water birds—a spotting scope may be a better choice than binoculars.
- Walk around groups of birds on the beach rather than forcing them to fly.
- Sit or crouch so that you appear smaller.
- Keep your movements slow and steady rather than fast or sporadic.
- If viewing from your car, stay in the car as long as possible. It acts as a viewing "blind" and the birds are less likely to fly if they don't recognize you as human.
- If you occasionally use recordings to attract birds, remember not to overuse them or to attract rare or protected species.

Birds will let you know if you are too close.

- Are you being dive-bombed by birds? Has a flock stopped feeding at your approach? Are the birds skittish? You're too close!

Beach nesting birds are masters of camouflage.

- Watch where you step—eggs and nests are nearly invisible against the backdrop of beach and dune, and young chicks may freeze in fear when danger approaches, rather than scurrying out from underfoot.
- Did you know? On a hot summer afternoon, temperatures at ground level on the beach can exceed 100 degrees Fahrenheit, dangerously high for exposed eggs or nestlings.
- Don't let curiosity get the best of you!

Respect private property boundaries, even if the bird you are following does not.

- Obey posted signs near nesting areas.

- Stay on roads, trails, and paths to minimize habitat disturbance.

- Traveler's tip: Resist the urge to drive your car on the beach, even if it's legal.

Does your backyard bird habitat get a four-star rating?

- Attract birds to a safe haven—keep dogs and cats confined.

- Always provide clean water and fresh bird seed.

- Promptly remove moldy bird seed and clean hummingbird feeders with hot water and vinegar every four or five days.

Map Key

1. Gannet Cluster
2. St. Marys Cluster
3. Kestrel Cluster
4. Painted Bunting Cluster
5. Upland Songbird Cluster
6. Limpkin Cluster
7. Warbler Hammocks Cluster
8. Swallow-Tailed Kite Cluster
9. Scrub-Jay Cluster
10. Tanager Cluster
11. Bittern and Bobwhite Cluster
12. River to Ocean Cluster
13. Natural Attractions Cluster
14. Turkey Cluster
15. Teal Cluster
16. Purple Gallinule Cluster
17. Ridge Cluster
18. Whooping Crane Cluster
19. Migrant Fallout Cluster
20. Vero Vireo Cluster
21. Scrub and Stream Cluster
22. Caracara Cluster
23. Sandhill Crane Cluster

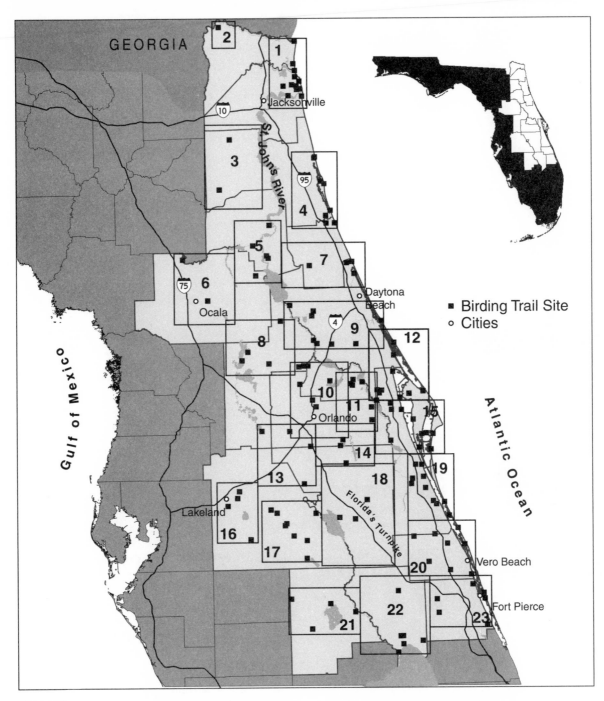

GEORGIA

Jacksonville

St. Johns River

Gulf of Mexico

Ocala

Daytona Beach

■ Birding Trail Site
○ Cities

Orlando

Atlantic Ocean

Lakeland

Florida's Turnpike

Vero Beach

Fort Pierce

City Locator
City / Map number

Bunnell 7
Cocoa 15
Daytona Beach 9
DeLeon Springs 9
Deltona 9
Fernandina Beach 1
Fort Pierce 23
Hilliard 2

Jacksonville 1, 3
Keystone Heights 3
Kissimmee 13
Lake Placid 21
Lake Wales 17
Lakeland 16
Leesburg 8
Melbourne 19

New Smyrna Beach 9, 12
Ocala 6
Okeechobee 22
Orlando 10, 13, 14
Ormond Beach 7
Oviedo 11
Palatka 5
Sebring 21

St. Augustine 4
St. Cloud 4, 18
Tavares 8
Titusville 12, 15
Vero Beach 20
Winter Haven 17

Legend

Not a primary Trail site, but "worth a visit" if you're already in an area

Site good for beginners

Some viewing is barrier-free

Tours, educational signage, and/or nature center on site

Entrance fee required

Seasonal hunting on site

Access by appointment only

Best time of day for birding: all day, both morning and evening, morning, evening

This site is primarily accessed, and birded, by car

This site is ONLY accessed by foot, and sometimes by bicycle

Recommended length of visit you should expect at a site: quick stop, a few hours, all day

This site is good for a single sought-after species

This site is good for seeing a variety of species

Restroom available

Gateway to the Great Florida Birding Trail

Fort Clinch State Park

Ann Morrow

Fort Clinch State Park is a crossroads: fresh water meets salt as the St. Marys River flows into the Atlantic; new meets old as modern naval submarines pass in front of the Civil War–era fort; dune ridge meets maritime hammock as one coastal habitat grades into another. And now, as a gateway to the Great Florida Birding Trail, Fort Clinch will bring together bird and birder. The bold colors of a painted bunting will turn the heads of some summer visitors. Others will be moved by winter birdscapes—perhaps a flock of bright-billed oystercatchers standing shoulder to shoulder on a sandbar, facing into a bitter wind.

Fort Clinch State Park anchors the northern tip of Amelia Island, Florida's northernmost Atlantic barrier island. From the ramparts of the restored fort, visitors can look north across Cumberland Sound, mixing zone for the Atlantic Ocean and the St. Marys River, to Georgia's Cumberland Island. The Amelia River and its salt marshes flank the park's western boundary; the Atlantic Ocean defines the easternmost. The southern edge of the park is Atlantic Avenue, lined with modest residential and commercial development, connecting to historic downtown Fernandina Beach.

A simple turn off Atlantic Avenue puts one on the long, winding Fort Clinch entrance road, a green tunnel through maritime forest. The limbs of live oaks, festooned with Spanish moss, arch overhead. Cabbage palm, red cedar, holly, and saw palmetto dominate the lush understory. During the spring and fall, the road provides an edge through this habitat, making it easy to look for tanagers, warblers, flycatchers, and orioles resting and feeding during their migratory flights through Florida. For the best experience, try a quiet early morning walk or bike ride along this passageway. On a summer evening stroll, listen for great-horned owl, chuck-will's-widow, and common nighthawk. The hammock is also the place to look for winter feeding guilds—mixed flocks of wintering birds such as the downy woodpecker, tufted titmouse, ruby-crowned kinglet, and yellow-throated, yellow-rumped, orange-crowned, and black-and-white warblers. Brown creeper, golden-crowned kinglet, and dark-eyed junco are rare winter treats.

As the park road threads its way north, it skirts the edge of Egans Creek marsh. It's worthwhile to pull over at designated spots and scan the marshes for conspicuous tall waders such as wood storks, great egrets, and great blue herons. In the winter, marsh wrens and sharp-tailed and seaside sparrows reward the patient observer.

The park's north end is where beach, pier, and open water host large numbers of birds. Terns, gulls, skimmers, oystercatchers, and plovers congregate on beach and sandbar. Binoculars will help you locate wintering loons, red-breasted mergansers, and horned grebes over open water. After a good storm, gannets and jaegers may get pushed in close to shore. Scan the rock jetty that parallels the pier for ruddy turnstones and one of the southernmost occurrences of wintering purple sandpipers.

The beach is the domain of two endangered and threatened species—the wintering piping plover and the summer-nesting least tern. These species are two very good reasons to practice a little birding etiquette: give feeding or roosting shorebirds a wide berth and remain vigilant for well-camouflaged shorebird nests.

Long before there was a fort or a state park on the part of Amelia Island known today as Fort Clinch State Park, birds visited and lived in its coastal habitats. They probe its sands, fish its waters, and feast on its acorns and wild grapes. They're at the Fort Clinch crossroads now. Don't miss them.

First Subsection Map

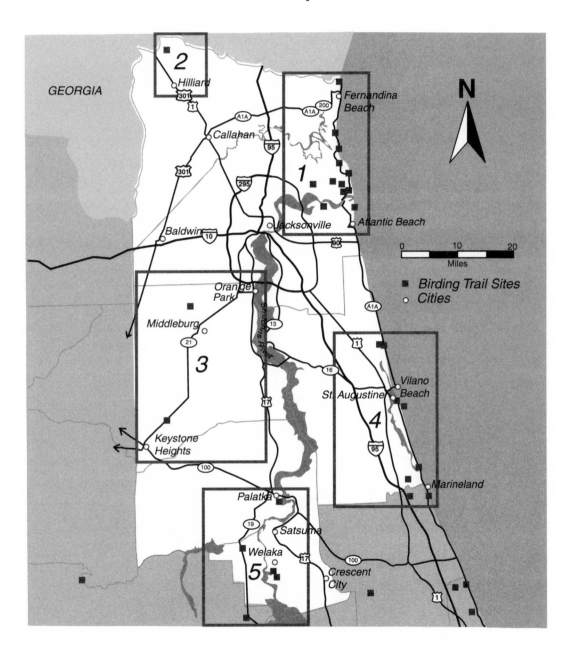

GEORGIA

2

Hilliard

Callahan

Baldwin

Fernandina Beach

Jacksonville

Atlantic Beach

1

Orange Park

Middleburg

3

Keystone Heights

St. Johns River

St. Augustine

Vilano Beach

4

Marineland

Palatka

Satsuma

Welaka

5

Crescent City

N

0   10   20
Miles

■ Birding Trail Sites
○ Cities

Gannet Cluster

1. Fort Clinch State Park 5

2. The Nature Center at Amelia Island Plantation 5

3. Amelia Island State Park 6

4. Big Talbot Island State Park 7

5. Little Talbot Island State Park 7

6. E. Dale Joyner Nature Preserve at Pelotes Island 8

7. Cedar Point 9

8. Kingsley Plantation 9

9. Fort George Island Cultural State Park 10

10. Huguenot Memorial Park 11

11. Fort Caroline National Memorial and Theodore Roosevelt Area 12

12. Kathryn Abbey Hanna Park 13

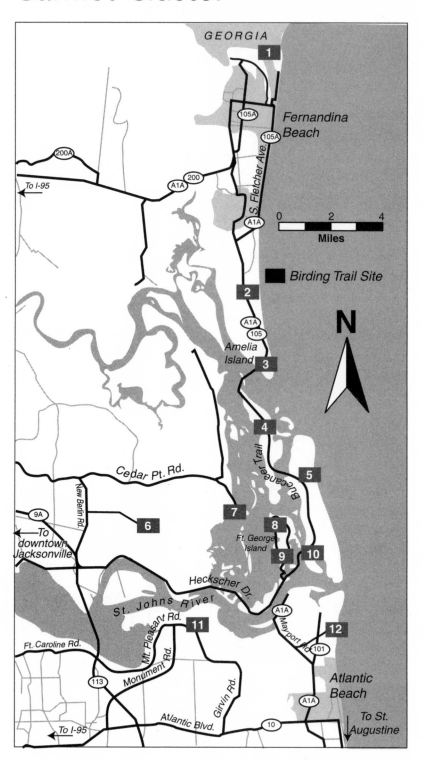

1. Fort Clinch State Park

DESCRIPTION: Northernmost gateway to the Great Florida Birding Trail, Fort Clinch would be in Georgia if it were any further north! It offers a great introduction to the breadth of Florida's bird species and nature habitats—from the migratory songbirds in its hammocks to the salt marshes filled with wading birds, to its beach and ocean covered with shorebirds and seabirds. On the canopy drive into the park, bird the hammock and neighboring marsh for warblers, waders, wrens, and sparrows. The visitor center at the Civil War–era fort has information on the birding trail, as does a pavilion display at the pier/jetty parking lot. Watch through the pavilion's bird window for painted buntings in spring and summer, and walk the pier for a vantage of the beach's terns, gulls, and shorebirds. Purple sandpipers frequent the fishing pier's jetty all winter; seabirds including harlequin ducks and all three scoters can sometimes be seen in the winter with a scope looking out to sea. The park offers nature walks every Saturday morning; call for details, or to schedule a tour for your group of fifteen or more.

DIRECTIONS: In Fernandina Beach, take A1A north to Atlantic Avenue. Turn left (west) and the park will be on the right (north) side of the road.

Open 8:00 A.M. to sunset. Best months for birding are January–May, September–December.

(904) 277-7274.

www.dep.state.fl.us/parks.

2. The Nature Center at Amelia Island Plantation

DESCRIPTION: The Nature Center at Amelia Island Plantation provides educational programs open to all, whether or not they are staying at the Plantation. Call ahead for a schedule of programs, or to schedule a customized program for your group! The Center offers everything from introductory birdwatching classes on-site to exciting off-site nature adventures. Appropriate for both children and adults, they provide an important complement— educational opportunities—to your birdwatching experience. On-site there is a black- and yellow-crowned night heron rookery, access to a salt marsh with views of shorebirds, painted buntings in their hammocks, and terns and gulls on their beaches. While not comparable to the adjacent natural areas offered in the Talbot Islands, they do provide a nice variety of species for practicing your beginning birding skills.

DIRECTIONS: The site is about ten miles south of Fernandina Beach on SR A1A. The Plantation is on the east side of the road north of the bridge to the Talbot Islands. Enter the Plantation's drive and inform the gatekeeper that you are visiting the Nature Center.

Open 9:00 A.M. to 5:00 P.M. Best months for birding are January–December.

(904) 321-5082.

www.aipfl.com.

3. Amelia Island State Park

DESCRIPTION: The state park on the southernmost tip of Amelia Island is worth a quick peek for shorebirds on the beach at low tide. Additionally, it offers an access to the catwalk on the bridge over Nassau Sound. From this point you can get a good look at the sandbars and bird islands in the sound—at low tide expect cormorants, pelicans, and migratory shorebirds to be loafing there—and see the birds flying to their roosts at sunset.

DIRECTIONS: This park is on the southernmost tip of Amelia Island, accessed by SR A1A.

Open 8:00 A.M. to sunset. Best months for birding are October–April.

(904) 251-2320.

www.dep.state.fl.us/parks.

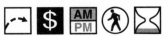

4. Big Talbot Island State Park

DESCRIPTION: Big Talbot Island State Park is one of a series of conservation lands along SR A1A on the north shore of the mouth of the St. Johns River. Check the cattail pond at the north tip of the island for shorebirds. This is excellent for Wilson's phalaropes in migration, along with avocets, black-necked stilts, and stilt sandpipers. Also check the marsh by the parking lot for rails. Further south, on the east side of the road, is the entrance for the Bluffs and Blackrock Trail, which give a vantage of the shoreline as well as islands in the pass where shorebirds, brown pelicans, and double-crested cormorants roost. Check the hammock along Blackrock for migratory songbirds in fall and spring, and for painted buntings in spring and summer. Maps for all the state park properties in this area may be picked up at the entrance station to Little Talbot Island State Park, south of this property on the southeast side of A1A.

DIRECTIONS: Big Talbot Island State Park is on A1A just south of Amelia Island.

Open 8:00 A.M. to sunset. Best months for birding are January–December.

(904) 251-2320.

www.dep.state.fl.us/parks.

5. Little Talbot Island State Park

DESCRIPTION: Little Talbot Island State Park is the center of the public lands on the north shore of the St. Johns River's outlet to the Atlantic. This should be your first stop before visiting the other sites in this complex—you can pick up bird lists and maps here, and learn of educational programming that may occur during your visit. Little Talbot is an excellent birding spot alone; be sure to ask at the ranger's station for recent painted bunting sightings in spring and early summer. The hiking trail to the north point is a great location to see buntings, and its hammocks are good for migratory songbirds in season. On the north point, loafing skimmers and terns are common, and large numbers of piping and Wilson's plovers and an occasional snowy plover feed in winter. Other beachgoers here and at neighboring Huguenot Park include seven sandpiper species, four plover species, red knots, dunlins, marbled godwits, and long-billed curlews. Watch offshore from the first beach boardwalk for Jacksonville's famed rare pelagics: jaegers and gannets are not unlikely! Educational programs are available for groups by advance reservation. Call for details.

DIRECTIONS: From I-95 in Jacksonville, take exit 124A (Heckscher Drive) east until you cross Fort George Inlet. From this point, Little Talbot Island State Park is three miles on your right.

Open 8:00 A.M. to sunset. Best months for birding are September–April.

(904) 251-2320.

www.dep.state.fl.us/parks.

6. E. Dale Joyner Nature Preserve at Pelotes Island

DESCRIPTION: A unique property, the Pelotes Island nature preserve is an educational opportunity provided by Jacksonville Electric Authority, Florida Power and Light, and the St. Johns River Power Park. Access is only in the form of group tours, which are provided by appointment. These free programs book months in advance, and cover topics from birding to Native American history. Birding tours, introductory birdwatching, and other environmental education programs are tailored to each group's request, free of charge. Individuals may request to join previously scheduled programs at the staff's discretion. The island's maritime hammock, salt marsh, and high-caliber programming make it a great introduction for beginning birdwatchers. Programs are offered October through April.

DIRECTIONS: Given upon confirmation of appointment.

Hours by appointment. Best months for birding are October–April.

(904) 665-8856.

http://pelotes.jea.com.

7. Cedar Point

DESCRIPTION: A gorgeous site, Cedar Point in the National Park Service's Timucuan Preserve features examples of maritime hammock, salt marsh, scrubby flatwoods, and freshwater wetland. It is a migrant magnet from mid-April through early May, and again from late September to mid-October, harboring painted and indigo buntings, rose-breasted grosbeaks, tanagers, and the gamut of warblers. This is one of the best places in Florida to observe yellow-breasted chats in the breeding season. Begin your exploration of this site at the boat basin, on the east side of the road, scanning for shore and wading birds, including sora and rails. Then enter the hiking trails on the west side of the road's end. Trails to the west and south end within a mile on the marsh front, but the northbound trail is longer and extends through some pine plantation areas and past some freshwater wetlands. This area is very wild—prepare to walk, and bring water. Yellow flies make this property unpleasant from late May to August.

DIRECTIONS: In Jacksonville, take Heckscher Drive east to New Berlin Road. Turn left (north) and follow New Berlin Road to Cedar Point Road. Turn right (east) and follow Cedar Point Road seven miles to the park at the end.

Open sunrise to sunset. Best months for birding are September–May.

(904) 241-3537.

www.nps.gov.

8. Kingsley Plantation

DESCRIPTION: Located on the tip of Fort George Island, the Kingsley Plantation is a good place in the Jacksonville area to view fall neotropical songbird migration. Mid-September to mid-October, birders will find ten-plus species of warblers, as well as wading birds, shorebirds, and raptors. Spring migration is equally exciting, with lots of black-throated blue warblers, ovenbirds, redstarts, and worm-eating warblers. A visitor center on-site details the cultural history of the property. Portions of this island are in private ownership. Please respect posted private property.

DIRECTIONS: From I-95 in Jacksonville, take Heckscher Drive east eighteen miles. Fort George Island will be on the left (north) side of the road half a mile past the St. Johns River Ferry Landing, and before Little Talbot Island State Park. Kingsley Plantation is on the island's northernmost tip.

Open 9:00 A.M. to 5:00 P.M. Best months for birding are October–April.

(904) 251-3537.

www.nps.gov.

9. Fort George Island Cultural State Park

DESCRIPTION: Fort George Island has two birding sites: the Cultural State Park and the National Park Service's Kingsley Plantation. When visiting the state park, drive the loop road through the hammock, looking for migrants in season and breeding buntings in spring and summer. Pick up a self-guiding tour book at the old clubhouse and take the foot trail across the street, birding for warblers, buntings, and other songbirds. The salt marsh is home to wading birds like snowy egrets and white ibis, and shorebirds loaf on exposed mud-flats in the pass. Portions of this island are in private ownership. Please respect posted private property.

DIRECTIONS: From I-95 in Jacksonville, take Heckscher Drive east eighteen miles. Fort George Island will be on the left (north) side of the road. After turning left, veer right on the loop road to the clubhouse where you can get information on the site and its trails.

Open 8:00 A.M. to sunset. Best months for birding are October–May.

(904) 251-2320.

www.dep.state.fl.us/parks.

10. Huguenot Memorial Park

DESCRIPTION: An oceanfront city park visited most often by fisherfolk and beachgoers, Huguenot Memorial Park is an incredibly attractive birding spot in its own right. Part of the park has been long designated as a critical wildlife area for nesting terns and shorebirds, and is roped off to protect these nesters in season. The beach is an important loafing site for terns, gulls, and skimmers by the hundreds, and a variety of shorebirds feed on exposed mudflats at low tide. In October it is one of the best spots in Florida to spot lesser black-backed gulls, and long-billed curlews are regular winter residents. Gannets, loons, and sea ducks can be seen in the distance from late fall through early spring. This site is well known for rare bird sightings: bar-tailed godwits (one sighting), snow buntings, lark sparrows, bridled terns, short-eared owls, and Lapland longspurs have all been seen in recent years. Beach driving is open for the more intrepid (and four-wheel-drive-equipped) birders. "Early bird" tickets can also be bought the day before for 6:00 A.M. entrance. From the entrance, drive into the park and leave your car before the beach access. Search the sheltered shallows on the north side of the peninsula for waders, shorebirds, and ducks. Following the beach around the tip, watch for loafing terns and gulls, and scope for birds out at sea.

DIRECTIONS: From I-95 in Jacksonville, take Heckscher Drive east seventeen miles. Huguenot Park is on the right (south) side of the road.

Open 8:00 A.M. to 6:00 P.M. (summers, 8:00 A.M. to 8:00 P.M.). Best months for birding are September–April.

(904) 251-3335.

www.coj.net/fun.

11. Fort Caroline National Memorial and Theodore Roosevelt Area

DESCRIPTION: These areas are part of the National Park Service's Timucuan Preserve, and represent some of the last untouched coastal habitat in northeast Florida. Stop in the visitor center at Fort Caroline for an introduction to the area and a map, then drive to the Theodore Roosevelt Area trailhead for a gorgeous hike through maritime hammock out to the salt marsh overlook. At this fabulous site for migratory songbirds, the thicker underbrush increases the likelihood of birds at eye level, rather than birding by ear for species up in the canopy. Summer is uncomfortably hot and buggy, but fall, winter, and spring promise pleasant hikes with spectacular birds including painted buntings, grosbeaks, orioles, and warblers.

DIRECTIONS: On the south side of the river east of downtown Jacksonville, take SR 10 east to Monument Road. Turn left (north) and proceed until Monument Road dead-ends in Fort Caroline Road. Turn right (east). Veer right on Fort Caroline Road to go to Fort Caroline National Monument Visitor Center, or veer right on Mount Pleasant Road to reach the Theodore Roosevelt Area trailhead, half a mile ahead on the left.

Open sunrise to sunset. Best months for birding are September–April.

(904) 641-7155.

www.nps.gov.

12. Kathryn Abbey Hanna Park

DESCRIPTION: A city beach park, Kathryn Abbey Hanna Park offers a diversity of habitats, although they can be heavily trafficked by visitors staying at the on-site campground. Park immediately after passing the entrance gate and walk south on the dirt road for a view of the freshwater finger lakes and their wading birds, anhingas, and a variety of waterfowl. The hardwood hammock northeast of the parking lot has bike trails where migratory songbirds are common in season. The park's bird list, available at the entrance station, includes a nice mix of forest, wading, and shorebirds. By driving farther into the park, you can access the beachfront, searching for shorebirds, terns, and gulls. Beach access 9 is equipped with a gazebo and fixed binocular scope to help you search the ocean for gannets, loons, sea ducks, and grebes. In winter the Jacksonville area is noted for its occasional sightings of the rarer pelagics, including both parasitic and pomarine jaegers, so keep your eyes peeled! Also, large flights of red-throated loons have been observed off Jacksonville beaches during recent winters.

DIRECTIONS: Take I-95 in Jacksonville to SR 10 (Atlantic Boulevard). Drive east to Mayport Road (A1A). Turn left (north) on Mayport Road and veer right on SR 101 when it diverges from A1A. Approximately three-quarters of a mile after the split, turn right (east) on Wonderwood Dr. The park is straight ahead.

Open 8:00 A.M. to 6:00 P.M. (summers, 8:00 A.M. to 8:00 P.M.). Best months for birding are September–April.

(904) 249-4700.

www.coj.net/fun.

Painted Buntings in Florida

The End of the Rainbow Holds No Gold

Jim Cox

Legend has it that painted buntings got their beautiful colors by mistake. The nature goddess gathered the birds to paint them, but she tripped over the peacock's tail and accidentally flung her magical palette into the air. The palette hit the ground next to the male bunting, colors splashed everywhere, and the bunting was shrouded with the most beautiful combination of hues ever seen.

Whether by design or accident, the painted bunting is surely the most spectacular of all North American birds. Males are so brilliantly colored—purple, blue, red, yellow, and green—that early naturalists named them nonpareil, or "without equal." And although females are more subtle, their green and yellow plumage reminds some of lemon-lime sherbet.

Unfortunately, sightings of this colorful bird are becoming rare. The painted bunting shows one of the sharpest population declines of any songbird, with a loss of 58 percent of the population in thirty years. If framed in terms of Florida's human population, the losses equal the disappearance of seven million people since 1970.

Such losses in the human race usually prompt herculean research efforts, but scientific work on buntings is in its infancy. We really do not know the underlying causes of the decline. Buntings breed along the Atlantic coast from northern Brevard County to the Georgia state line. Loss of coastal habitats to development is certainly high on the list of possible causes, since about 70 percent of Florida's human population lives near the coast.

Another suspect is a drab bird at the opposite end of the color spectrum from buntings: brown-headed cowbirds. Cowbirds drop their eggs in other birds' nests and let the foster parents raise young cowbirds. Once hatched, young cowbirds are not kind to their nestmates, either. Cowbirds often kick legitimate nestlings overboard or outcompete them for food. Sightings of adult buntings feeding young cowbirds are commonplace along Florida's Atlantic coast.

Biologists also worry about homeless feral cats, since these have devastated wildlife populations found near residential and urban development. The large human population associated with Florida's coastal areas surely implies a large feral cat population.

And if these assaults weren't enough, the decline also may be attributed to the pet trade outside the United States. Birds, painted buntings among them, migrate to south Florida and parts of the West Indies in winter, and many birds are trapped and sold as pets.

Concern for buntings runs high because their Atlantic coast breeding range hugs a narrow band that does not go far inland. This means that painted buntings can be eliminated much more quickly than other declining songbirds whose breeding ranges cover larger areas.

Biologists also worry that the full impact of the decline has not been properly framed. Painted buntings occur in the western United States, but recent work has shown that eastern and western buntings are very distinct beasts. The populations are genetically isolated and have developed different songs, migration routes, and molting patterns. We may be losing more than an isolated population of colorful birds; we may be losing a unique species.

Fortunately, buntings have not declined to the point that birders have great difficulty locating these bright splashes of color. Buntings can be found at many state parks and wildlife management areas from approximately Fort Pierce northward. Look for them in shrubby patches of oak, along the edges of oak hammocks, and in open brush.

Painted buntings are small, chromatic symphonies that brighten up any field trip, but a dark cloud hangs over their future. Unless more attention is focused on the riddle of bunting decline, we someday may see an end to their rainbow.

Birds at Sea, Birders on the Coast

Noel Wamer

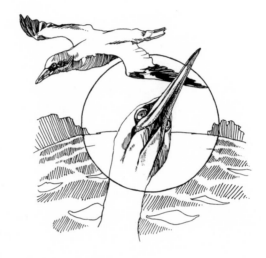

Many birders think of jaegers as mysterious birds, seldom seen from dry land. And it's true, these seafaring birds nest only in the Arctic and spend their nonbreeding seasons ranging the world's oceans. Just the mention of jaegers brings to mind rigorous, and frequently uncomfortable, offshore trips aboard small boats in search of them. The most recent comprehensive accounts of Florida's bird life state that they are rarely seen from land. However, through regular "sea watches" in recent years, I have found that both pomarine and parasitic jaegers can be regularly observed from shore in northeast Florida, establishing our area as one the best places to look for these birds in North America (see Gannet Cluster).

The sea watch season runs from mid-October through early April, and jaegers appear off the northeast Florida coast in early November and remain through March. The time of day does not seem to matter much. Since you will be looking toward the east, lighting conditions are best in the afternoon. Still, at this time of year, the sun is far enough to the south to permit successful morning sea watching.

I sea watch from a number of locations along the coast, from Fort Clinch State Park (site 1) in Fernandina Beach south to Vilano Beach in St. Johns County, and observe jaegers at all locations. Perhaps the best, because of its height above the water, is the observation deck at the north beach access of Guana River State Park in northern St. Johns County (sites 16 and 17). The best technique for locating jaegers is to visit a number of locations, concentrating on those where shrimp boats are working close to shore.

An apparent myth about jaegers and other pelagic species is that they are seen most often from land during storms. While this may be true for some pelagic species, I find rough weather is the worst time to look for jaegers. Strong winds and storm-driven waves create surface refraction that severely limits visibility; moreover, the birds do not come as close to shore during bad weather.

The pursuit of sea watching in northeast Florida will allow you to observe many interesting species in addition to jaegers, some of them uncommon to rare in Florida. Other than gulls and terns, the most conspicuous species I observe during my watches are northern gannets, frequently by the hundreds. Throughout the fall and early winter, a remarkable passage of thousands of ducks occurs. Most travel in long lines, passing too far offshore to be identified, but you can expect to see scoters, almost all blacks. In spring, a very interesting and little-known northbound movement of herons and egrets can be observed watching out at sea. Some real rarities seen during 1999–2001 sea watches were red-throated loons, great cormorants, and long-tailed ducks.

I hope that this short account of the sea watching possibilities in northeast Florida will excite you enough to get out and try this interesting form of birding. Don't forget that you will need a good telescope: although jaegers and other birds may sometimes come in as close as the onshore breakers, typically they fly farther out. A folding chair will be useful at some locations. Last, but certainly not least, be prepared for some frustration. Jaegers are notoriously difficult to identify because of their complex combinations of age and color variations. But with patience and careful size comparisons to the nearby gulls and terns, you should be able to sort some of them out!

An on-line guide to sea watch locations:
http://www.badbirdz.com/seawatchIndex.htm.
On-line weather information:
www.ndbc.noaa.gov/Maps/Florida.shtml.

St. Marys Cluster

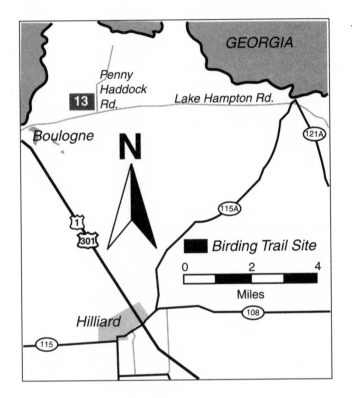

13. Ralph E. Simmons State Forest   20

13. Ralph E. Simmons State Forest

DESCRIPTION: The remote and wild Simmons State Forest is separated from Georgia by the St. Marys River, and offers some rustic hiking through sandhill and slope-forest habitats down to the river itself. Stop at the check station trailhead on Penny Haddock Road to check for hunt dates and to pick up a map. Then drive another mile to a second entrance on the left side. This road leads three miles down to White Sand Landing. Along the way you may see bobwhite, sparrows, and turkeys, along with migrants like kinglets, vireos, warblers, and kites, and finally waterbirds at the river's edge. Miles of other trails crisscross the forest, providing the opportunity to hike as far as you like. Another excellent birding experience is to canoe the river; you can rent canoes from a private concession at the corner of US 1 and Lake Hampton Road. From the river in springtime you may see everything from mottled ducks to swallow-tailed kites to nesting prothonotary warblers. The river is a popular recreation spot in warm months, so for undisturbed birding, visit in the mornings or on weekdays.

DIRECTIONS: From Hilliard in western Nassau County, take US 1 (SR 301) north six miles to Boulogne. Turn right (east) on Lake Hampton Road, go two miles, and turn left (north) on Penny Haddock Road. The entrance to the forest will be on the left (west) side of the road.

Open sunrise to sunset. Best months for birding are January, May–March, September–November. Area closed to birders during hunting season.

(904) 693-5055.

www.fl-dof.com.

Kestrel Cluster

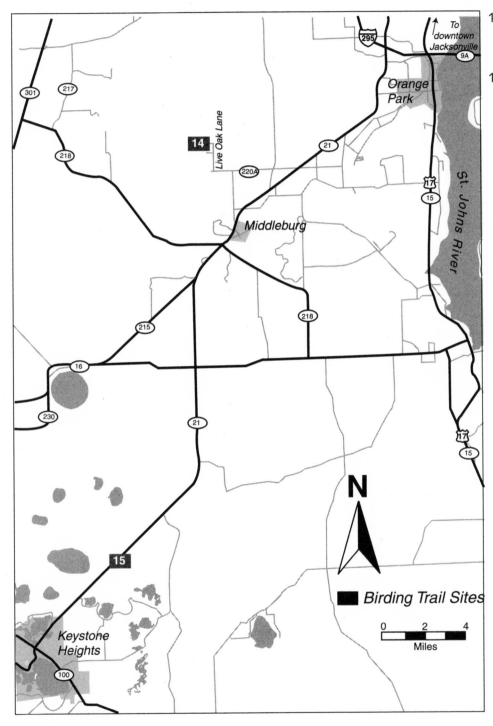

14. Jennings State Forest 22

15. Mike Roess Gold Head Branch State Park 23

14. Jennings State Forest

DESCRIPTION: A little-known wild area, Jennings State Forest provides some excellent opportunities for sandhill species, including Bachman's sparrows, brown-headed nuthatches, kestrels, red-headed woodpeckers, and nighthawks. Stop at the North Fork Black Creek trailhead on Live Oak Lane to pick up a map and trail guide. Woodpeckers and nuthatches are likely on this loop. The viewing tower at the power line at the end of the road is especially good for Bachman's sparrows, kestrels, and bluebirds. Birding by ear helps at this site, although beginners will enjoy hiking the habitats, if not identifying all the birds. There is hunting on this property in the fall and spring; check trailheads or call for dates/closures. Guided birding walks are available by appointment.

DIRECTIONS: Take SR 21 southeast six miles from Orange Park. Turn right (west) on Old Jennings Road (220A). Turn north on Live Oak Lane. Trailheads will be on the left (west) side of the road.

Open sunrise to sunset. Best months for birding are October–April.

(904) 291-5530.

www.fl-dof.com.

15. Mike Roess Gold Head Branch State Park

DESCRIPTION: The unusual Gold Head Branch park provides access into a unique ravine slope-forest, popular in season with migratory songbirds including tanagers, thrushes, orioles, and warblers. Red-headed woodpeckers use standing snags in the area, and eagles and swallow-tailed kites frequent the park's lakes. Turkeys and bobwhite are common in the morning along the road through the sandhill on the drive into the park, as are kestrels and other raptors. Check the lakefronts for wading birds, ducks, and terns. By camping on-site, you can have access to the property at night to prowl for owls, as well as early in the morning before the entrance station admits the general public. For scheduled programs and events, call in advance for details and reservations.

DIRECTIONS: From Keystone Heights take SR 21 northeast six miles. Park is on the right (east) side of the road.

Open 8:00 A.M. to sunset. Best months for birding are January–December.

(352) 473-4701.

www.dep.state.fl.us/parks.

Fall Migration of Raptors

Why, When, and Where

Matthew Mullenix

I am but mad north-north-west: when the wind is
Southerly I know a hawk from a handsaw.

William Shakespeare, *Hamlet,* **II.2**

Something in the beat of a raptor's wing naturally draws the eye. Even at a distance, the dark shape and spirited flight of a hawk or falcon are immediately recognizable. From our vantage at the crest of a small hill, my friend points low near the horizon, mutters a quiet "There's one," and the race is on to name the fast approaching bird.

It's a small hawk, dashing between sand dunes and saw palmettos, difficult to see. The bird is smaller than a Cooper's hawk and flying too close to cover for a kestrel. Its size and speed suggest a sharp-shinned hawk or a merlin indulging in an early hunting flight. For my money, it's a merlin. I nearly say so out loud when the bird is upon us. We drop our binoculars and watch the young female sharp-shinned hawk glide over our position. My companion nods. "Thought so."

Friendly competition and a chance to hone one's identification skills are among the attractions of watching birds of prey on migration. Simply seeing them is a thrill for many: raptors are typically solitary and thinly distributed over wide areas. Watching dozens, even hundreds, of hawks and falcons at once is a rare pleasure.

With more than eight hundred miles of shoreline along the Eastern Continental Flyway, Florida has much to offer the migratory raptor enthusiast. Owing to the funneling effect at the state's southern extremity, the highest concentrations of ospreys, eagles, hawks, and falcons will pass through the Florida Keys, but northeastern Florida is a less remote birding prospect.

Near Jacksonville, visit Amelia Island State Park (site 3) and Big Talbot Island State Park (site 4). Both provide a combination of beach, marsh, and woodland attractive to a variety of raptors. Following the raptors' migration south, visit Guana River Wildlife Management Area and State Park (sites 16 and 17), a twelve-thousand-acre coastal "magnet" for wintering shorebirds and waterfowl and, by association, for a host of migrant birds of prey. Though most raptors migrate along Florida's coasts, inland areas are also worth a look. Broad-winged and rough-legged hawks have been sighted at Emeralda Marsh (sites 38 and 39) and Sunnyhill Restoration Area (site 37).

Wherever you decide to look for migrating birds of prey, timing will be critical. Raptor movement through coastal Florida will immediately precede and follow a cold front, so some of the best days for big flights are the worst for picnics: cold, wet, and windy. There's no reason to let precipitation keep you home. Peregrines will fly in half a gale and a stinging pelt of rain. Choosing the right weeks to observe is also important. Birds migrate from August through November, but each species tends to peak regionally during a certain period. In northeastern Florida, osprey start early and may be seen in August, September, and October. Merlins are among the first falcons to arrive, starting in mid-September, and are followed closely by American kestrels. All the falcons, including the peregrine, will peak within the first three weeks of October. Accipiters (Cooper's and sharp-shinned hawks), harriers, and buteos (the broad-winged, red-tailed, and red-shouldered hawks) are flying well at this time too, though they peak somewhat later in October.

For the best chance of a large flight and a variety of species, choose a cloudy to clearing October day on the heels of a strong cold front, with brisk winds from the northerly quarter. Start at sunrise, looking for a flash of wing against the salt marsh, a dark shape hugging the ground and flying fast. But until you're certain, don't tell your friend what sort of hawk you think you see.

Painted Bunting Cluster

16. Guana River Wildlife Management Area   27

17. Guana River State Park   27

18. St. Augustine Alligator Farm   28

19. Anastasia State Park   29

20. Fort Matanzas National Monument   29

21. Faver-Dykes State Park   30

22. Princess Place Preserve   31

23. Washington Oaks Gardens State Park   32

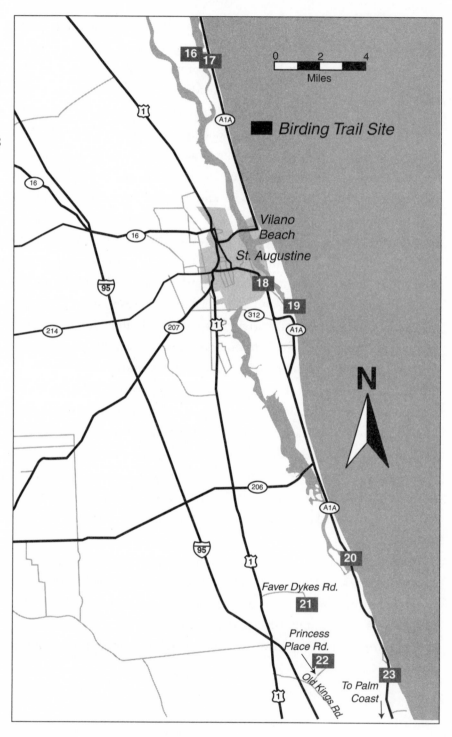

16. Guana River Wildlife Management Area

DESCRIPTION: The wildlife management area is a great complement to the adjacent Guana River State Park. More rustic and wild than its neighbor to the south, it offers twelve miles of hiking trails (round-trip) through flatwoods, oak hammocks, scrub, and wetlands. Two overlooks, one on Capo Creek and one on Lake Ponte Vedra, give good vantages of duck populations, for which the area is known, as well as egrets, herons, and spoonbills. During hunts on Thursdays through Sundays, October through January, birders can drive in with automobiles, making the area significantly more accessible. Simply check in at the check station for a drive-in pass. At other times, birders need to park at the dam and hike or bike in, veering right on the west side of the dam and heading north into the wildlife management area. Watch for migratory songbirds in the hammocks as well as owls and woodpeckers. Duck concentrations are highest—where else?—in the northernmost, and most remote, part of Lake Ponte Vedra. Pick up a map, bring a bottle of water, and tie on your hiking shoes. This site makes you work for your birds, but the rewards are well worth it.

DIRECTIONS: From St. Augustine, take SR A1A north through Vilano Beach. The site is eight miles north, on the left (west) side of the road. Enter through the state park, parking on the dam and hiking across the dam and north into the wildlife management area. The property may also be entered from the Roscoe Boulevard Extension entrance at the north end of the management area.

Open sunrise to sunset. Best months for birding are October–May.

(904) 825-6877.

17. Guana River State Park

DESCRIPTION: Guana River is an all-day affair! Most notably, this is a first-class site for viewing the fall peregrine falcon migration. Visit the tower on the beach side of A1A and sit patiently during the first two weeks of October. Falcons migrate south, following the dune line and feeding on shorebirds as they go, putting on a quite a show for viewers who flock here to watch and count them each year. This overlook also offers one of the best vantages in Florida to scope out at sea for pomarine and parasitic jaegers, which inevitably taunt you just beyond your optics' capabilities. At the entrance to the east side of the park, bird the dam for shorebirds, clapper rails, ducks, loons, and grebes. Bobolinks like the fallow area leading up to the hiking trails in fall and spring, when the hammocks are thick with warblers, buntings, grosbeaks, and other songbirds too. Hike out to the western shoreline to look for shorebirds or, better yet, hike the two miles to the southernmost point, where plovers and oystercatchers loaf on shell spits and forage in the inlet's rich waters. Wading birds enjoy the wetland in the interior of the property; scan for egrets, herons, and bitterns. Educational programs, including bird walks, occur regularly, so call ahead for a schedule of activities. The site's impressive bird list is available at the office just east of the dam.

DIRECTIONS: From St. Augustine, take SR A1A north through Vilano Beach. Guana River State Park is eight miles north, on both sides of the road.

Open 8:00 A.M. to sunset. Best months for birding are January–December.

(904) 825-5071.

www.dep.state.fl.us/parks.

18. St. Augustine Alligator Farm

DESCRIPTION: Because of the alligators resident at this attraction, wading birds like snowy egrets, great egrets, wood storks, and tricolored herons have long nested above the American alligators. Why would they nest over such a threat? Because the alligators provide them with protection from raiders like raccoons, who would gladly eat eggs and chicks in their nests. Boardwalks through this facility wind through the rookery, giving an up-close look at birds, their nests, and their young that is great for photographers and viewers alike. The birds are very habituated to people on the boardwalks and are not disturbed by viewers approaching to distances of an arm's length. While some birds are almost always nesting at this site, the peak falls between April and July, with great blue herons beginning earlier and black-crowned night herons finishing up the breeding season. One benefit to buying a member pass is early morning access to the site before the general public—perfect for photography and nature study. Call ahead or ask on site for details.

DIRECTIONS: From I-95, exit at SR 16 and drive east seven miles to SR A1A. Turn right on A1A and cross the Bridge of Lions onto Anastasia Island. The site is a mile and a half ahead on the right (west) side of the road.

Open 9:00 A.M. to 5:00 P.M. Best months for birding are March–September.

(904) 824-3337.

www.alligatorfarm.com.

19. Anastasia State Park

DESCRIPTION: Anastasia has it all—beachfront, sheltered wetlands, and maritime hammock. On the way in, bird the salt run for wading birds and rails, then hike the trail by the campground looking in the maritime hammock for likely painted buntings in spring and summer and migrating warblers in April and October. The beachfront offers a look for terns, gulls, sandpipers, and plovers. Walk, bike, or drive (if you have four-wheel drive) to the north point of the beach for a better diversity of shorebirds and terns. Scope offshore for sea ducks, common and red-throated loons, cormorants, gannets, and occasional pelagics like jaegers. Bikes are available for rent on-site.

DIRECTIONS: From I-95, exit at SR 207. Take SR 207 northeast to CR 312, turn right (east), and proceed to SR A1A. Turn left (north) on SR A1A. The park is approximately two miles north on the right (east) side of the road.

Open 8:00 A.M. to sunset. Best months for birding are January–December.

(904) 461-2000.

www.dep.state.fl.us/parks.

20. Fort Matanzas National Monument

DESCRIPTION: Fort Matanzas National Monument encompasses the southern tip of Anastasia Island adjacent to the Matanzas Inlet. Several birding areas are available. You can park at the beach entrance on the west side of A1A just before the Matanzas bridge and walk the inlet shore looking for shorebirds like semipalmated plovers foraging along the wrack line and spotted sandpipers compulsively bobbing their tails, or scope the river for ducks like redbreasted and hooded mergansers, as well as loons and grebes. On the ocean side, terns and gulls become more abundant, and the opportunity to spot plunging gannets and other pelagic birds arises. Four-wheel driving is allowed on the beach, if you so choose. Watch these parking areas and dunes for painted buntings in spring and summer. The visitor center is located 0.3 miles north of these beach accesses on the west side of the road. At this point you can pick up an area map and a bird list and hike the boardwalk nature trail through maritime hammock, watching for neotropical migrants and buntings. Guided bird walks are scheduled regularly, so call ahead for details and reservations before your visit.

DIRECTIONS: From I-95, exit at CR 206 and go east six miles to SR A1A. Turn right (south) and follow A1A four miles to Fort Matanzas National Monument. The visitor center will be on the right (west) side of the road, with more beach accesses 0.3 miles ahead before the Matanzas Inlet bridge.

Beach open twenty-four hours a day, visitor center open 9:00 A.M. to 4:30 P.M. daily. Best months for birding are January–December.

(904) 471-0116.

21. Faver-Dykes State Park

DESCRIPTION: The rustic Faver-Dykes site has trails winding through thick maritime hammock and flatwoods and along an extensive salt marsh. A raw, gorgeous piece of native Florida, it (or at least its biting insects) is not for the faint of heart. Its breathtaking habitats harbor a diversity of neotropical migrants, however, and birders able to identify birdsongs will have a banner day during migrations. Check the estuary for waders, eagles, white pelicans, migratory ducks, and clapper rails. This is probably a site most appreciated by the thick-skinned lister with good birding-by-ear skills. Its aesthetics are rapturous to even the novice, however, and warrant a quick drive through, if you happen to be in the area.

DIRECTIONS: From I-95 north of Palm Coast, take US 1 half a mile north to Faver Dykes Road. Turn right (east) and drive a mile and a half to the park entrance at the end.

Open 8:00 A.M. to sunset. Best months for birding are October–April.

(904) 794-0997.

www.dep.state.fl.us/parks.

22. Princess Place Preserve

DESCRIPTION: Princess Place Preserve on the Matanzas River offers access to a freshwater creek, salt marsh, oak hammock, and flatwoods habitats. This is the site of an old homestead, and there are still historic homes, an artesian fountain, and a few private inholdings on the property. Several hiking and driving trails wind through the site. Upon entering, watch for turkeys and bobwhite by the roadside, and stop at the first trail on the left for hiking access to the marsh. Watch for wading birds, foraging shorebirds, and ducks; snipe and woodcock are also likely. Across the creek, the next trailhead on the left leads to some more xeric (drier) habitats—watch for raptors and woodpeckers in the open areas leading to the trail. Flycatchers also frequent this entrance area, preying on hapless insects before your eyes. Finally, when the road reaches the waterfront, it winds to the right around a private inholding and ends at the green trail, which gives access to good neotropical migratory songbird habitat. The green trail ends by circling an old artesian fountain, around which great egrets and blue herons nest in season. Please be careful not to disturb nesting and resting birds, and respect the private property within this preserve.

DIRECTIONS: From the intersection of US 1 and I-95 north of Palm Coast, take US 1 south about two miles to Old Kings Road. Turn left (east) and travel a mile and a half to Princess Place Road. Turn left (northeast) and drive approximately two miles into the preserve.

Open Wednesday through Sunday, 9:00 A.M. to 5:00 P.M. Best months for birding are October–April.

(386) 446-7630.

23. Washington Oaks Gardens State Park

DESCRIPTION: Washington Oaks Gardens stretches from the ocean to the Matanzas River. Check the beachfront for shorebirds, the surf for loons, grebes, and sea ducks, and offshore for gannets. This beach is a good place to view the fall raptor migration from the end of September to the beginning of October. Then cross the street and explore the riverside property: After passing the entrance gate, the road curves to the south. At this curve, a trail takes off to the north, bound for scrub and xeric hammock. Following the road to the south will take you past the ornamental gardens through some oak hammock. You can bird the road for neotropical songbird migrants in season, or take the hammock trail from the last picnic area north to the visitor center. Part of the cultivated waterfront can still be good for shorebirds (watch for spotted sandpipers and their telltale tail bobbing!) and gives a good vantage of exposed sand spits in the river where shorebirds, gulls, terns, and waders loaf and feed. Watch for a diversity of ducks in the river in fall and winter also. Washington Oaks hosts an Earth Day celebration each April, and the local Audubon chapter leads occasional bird walks. Check at the entrance gate for more info. While driving A1A near this park, watch the coastal scrub for Florida scrub-jays!

DIRECTIONS: Take I-95 to SR 100 in Flagler County. Drive SR 100 east to SR A1A in Flagler Beach. Turn north on A1A and go twelve miles to Washington Oaks State Gardens. Beach access will be on your right (east); the park entrance station, with maps and bird list, on your left (west).

Open 8:00 A.M. to sunset. Best months for birding are September–April.

(386) 446-6780.

www.dep.state.fl.us/parks.

Birdwatching 101

Identification Basics

Jim Cox

Birdwatching in Florida—be prepared for awe, astonishment, bug bites, and frustration. The first two pleasures will wash over you unexpectedly, even if you're a veteran birder. The frustration will diminish as you gain experience. And the bug bites—well, they're just something you always prepare for in this climate. To start you on the road to a lifetime of pleasurable birding, study the tips we present here, grab your binoculars, and head outdoors.

During your first few months of birdwatching, there are two general rules to keep in mind: (1) eliminate as many species as possible from consideration before you ever attempt to identify anything, and (2) the bird you see is most likely a species that commonly occurs in your area, not some strange exotic that blew in from a thousand miles away.

These rules are closely tied to one another, and they focus on making birding easier by reducing the number of choices you have to consider. One of the easiest ways to exclude birds is to go through your field guide and put an "X" next to those that do not typically occur in your geographical area. Put these aside for the time being. By doing this you drastically reduce the number of birds you have to worry about identifying, since there are some 300–400 birds that are regularly seen in Florida!

Another way to eliminate choices is to consider the time of year the bird might occur in your area. The range maps included with field guides help determine whether a bird is common or rare, migratory or residential in your area. A good checklist of Florida birds will help: check out the Resources section of this book for some suggestions. Those procedures will quickly eliminate a lot of confusing birds from consideration. For example, there are approximately 180 birds that breed in Florida and another 20 or so that hang around in small numbers during the summer. So if you see some unknown bird in the middle of July, you don't need to consider each of the 700 species shown in your field guide. Instead, you only have to choose from 200 or so different birds.

The way some birds skulk about, you'd think that they were afraid of showing off their pretty colors and didn't want anyone to identify them. Despite birds' shyness, however, there are five basic clues you can look and listen for that will allow you to solve the bird identification puzzle: (1) the bird's silhouette, (2) its plumage and coloration, (3) its behavior, (4) its habitat preferences, and (5) its voice. This may seem like a formidable amount of information to gather, but in truth you often need only one or two of these clues to identify a bird.

The mere outline of a bird is sometimes all that's needed to know which bird you're seeing. For example, from a silhouette you can tell whether a bird is large or small, short-legged or long-legged, crested or not crested, plump and roly-poly or slim and sleek, long-billed or short-billed, short-tailed or long-tailed, and so forth.

Plumage characteristics are what really draw a lot of people into birdwatching—they like seeing those pretty colors. The distinguishing plumage clues that identify different species are known as field marks, and these include such things as breast spots, wing bars (thin lines along the wings), eye rings (circles around the eyes), and of course coloration. Many field marks are concentrated around the head, so don't worry about checking the more hidden parts of a bird's anatomy. Pay particular attention to whether or not there is a dark line running "through" the eye (an eye line), a stripe above the eyebrow, whiskers along the side of the face, or a cap on top of the head.

A bird's behavior—how it flies, forages, or generally comports itself—is one of the best clues to its identity. Hawks, for example, have a "serious" demeanor, crows and jays are "gregarious," and cuckoos are . . . well, not really. Woodpeckers climb up the sides of tree trunks searching for grubs like a lineman scaling a telephone pole. Flycatchers, on the other hand, wouldn't climb a tree trunk if their lives depended on it. Even the way a bird props its tail gives some clues as to which species or family it might be.

Even though a bird occurs in your neck of the woods, this doesn't mean the bird will be common wherever you go. Birds segregate themselves according to habitat type and are sometimes quite picky in selecting an area as home. Beginning birdwatchers must usually spend many hours afield before they are able to associate different species with different habitat types. I suggest that you develop a key to habitats that you frequent and keep notes of where you see different species.

I've often thought it would be rewarding to teach blind people how to "bird listen." Most birds have unique songs and calls, and once you've gained a few years of experience, voice is all that's needed to identify many of the birds you encounter. Birdcalls are a form of advertisement that is usually directed specifically to other members of the species. If each species didn't have a distinctive call or song, there would be a lot of confusion out there. Some people find that listening to tapes and records helps them to learn the calls of birds. However, nothing helps you learn a call better than hearing the call, finding the bird that makes the noise, and then simply watching the bird sing for a moment. There's something about the association of voice and bird that helps to fix both in memory.

Here are a few other tips to help speed you along the bird identification learning curve. Take a field trip with groups offering bird tours throughout Florida. Use regional birding books, such as *A Birder's Guide to Florida* by Bill Pranty or this guide.

Birding is not the easiest sport in the world to learn but is definitely one of the most rewarding. To offset those first outings when you flip through your field guide in frustration, there will be many years' worth of pleasant and intriguing field trips. You see, birders learn something new every time they go out. If they don't actually see a new species for the first time, they might see a familiar bird do some new trick. They might even come across something startling, like a rare European bird that somehow strayed far from home. The constant variety and challenge of birding are two important attractions, but so too is the camaraderie. There are lots of people poking their heads into bushes and craning their necks toward the sky. I've developed a good number of lasting friendships as I've cruised some isolated road and happened across a kindred soul bedecked with binoculars and a field guide.

Remember, you're never alone when you're a birder.

This essay has been excerpted from *Bird Watching Basics,* available from the Florida Fish and Wildlife Conservation Commission, 620 South Meridian Street, Tallahassee, Florida, 32399-1600. The full text, also available at http://floridabirdingtrail.com/Birdbasics.htm, includes excellent information on the specifics of choosing field guides and binoculars.

Upland Songbird Cluster

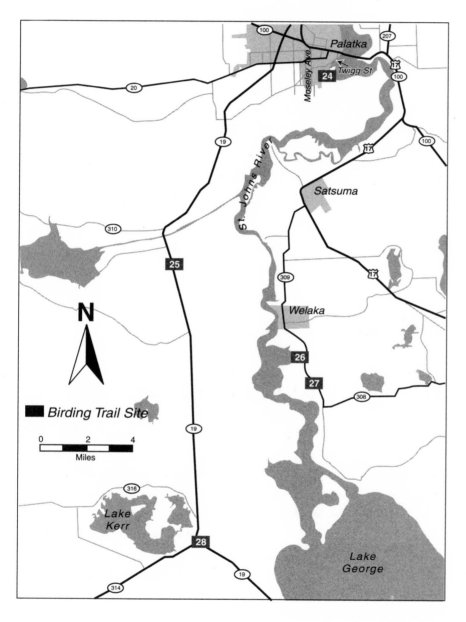

24. Ravine Gardens
    State Park   38

25. Caravelle Ranch
    Wildlife Manage-
    ment Area   38

26. Welaka State
    Forest   39

27. Welaka National
    Fish Hatchery and
    Aquarium   40

28. Ocala National
    Forest: Salt Springs
    41

24. Ravine Gardens State Park

DESCRIPTION: The remarkable topography makes a visit to the Ravine Gardens State Park interesting, regardless of the birding. Hike the ravine or drive the loop road around it, watching for migratory songbirds in season, such as cedar waxwings at the amphitheater in April, as well as resident woodpeckers, owls and hawks. Ruby-throated hummingbirds frequent the gardens in spring and summer, and the pond at the bottom of the ravine can have ducks and some wading birds. This site gets very busy in February and March when people flock to see the azaleas bloom. Visit early in the morning, and on weekdays, during these months.

DIRECTIONS: From SR 17 in Palatka, turn south on Moseley Avenue. Go to Twigg Street and turn left (east). Park entrance will be on your right.

Open 7:30 A.M. to sunset. Best months for birding are October–April.

(386) 329-3721.

www.dep.state.fl.us/parks.

25. Caravelle Ranch Wildlife Management Area

DESCRIPTION: If you're driving SR 19 south of Palatka, Caravelle Ranch Wildlife Management Area is worth a quick peek. If your visit falls during a hunting season between September and March, you are free to drive into the area, where you will likely see sparrows and turkeys, wading birds and swallow-tailed kites along the slough. Stop at the check station for a map of the area to best plan your tour. If your visit falls outside of hunting season, there is a walk-through entrance to the property about a mile south of the check station/main entrance on the east side of the road. This hiking trail leads through a hammock where you can watch for songbird migrants in October and April. You may also enter through walk-in gates at the main entrance.

DIRECTIONS: Take SR 19 south from Palatka approximately ten miles. The main entrance is about a mile south of the Barge Canal bridge on the left (east) side of the road.

Open sunrise to sunset. Best months for birding are October–April.

(386) 329-2517.

26. Welaka State Forest

DESCRIPTION: If you're already visiting the Welaka National Fish Hatchery, you should stop by Welaka State Forest's trails. From the parking area south of their headquarters, a paved Talking Tree Trail offers good interpretation on the habitats and wildlife of the forest. The boardwalk also extends out into the floodplain forest of the St. Johns River, which could be good for migratory songbirds like indigo buntings and black-and-white warblers in October and again in April. The John's Landing hiking trail extends to the south for more than four and a half miles' worth of hiking. Expect turkeys, bobwhite, some mixed flocks of migrating warblers, and sandhill cranes nesting in the ephemeral wetlands. Bald eagles nest nearby and are frequently seen flying over the property. The Mud Spring Trail is 1.7 miles long, and its entrance is north of the Talking Tree Trail. Its birdwatching characteristics are good, but it is heavily traveled, so unless you are birding on a weekday morning, you may not see much. Be sure to pick up a hiking trail map at the entrance kiosk or at the forest office. This is a remote area—carry water and expect heat and insects in summer.

DIRECTIONS: From Palatka, take SR 17 south twenty miles to CR 309. Go west on CR 309 to Welaka. Continue on CR 309. Office will be half a mile south of Welaka on the left (east) side of the road. Mud Spring Trail is on the right (west) side of the road. Go one mile further south and the Talking Tree Trail and John's Landing trailhead will be on the right (west) side of the road.

Open sunrise to sunset. Best months for birding are October–April.

(386) 467-2388.

www.fl-dof.com

27. Welaka National Fish Hatchery and Aquarium

DESCRIPTION: The Welaka hatchery is used by the United States Fish and Wildlife Service to raise fish for stocking programs. The production ponds where they hatch and raise the young fish have drawn attention from fish-eating wading birds for years, but rather than discourage the birds, the hatchery has instead set up a viewing platform for birders! When water is in the ponds, you can view eagles and osprey, egrets and herons of all kinds, wood storks, kingfishers, and hooded mergansers feeding in the ponds. Additionally, hike the three-quarter-mile nature trail just north of the observation tower for migratory woodland species and turkeys. Check the wires around the parking area for eastern bluebirds too. An aquarium showcasing the hatchery's program is located one mile north of the observation tower, on the east side of the road. The hatchery also offers excellent tours to groups, visiting the birding areas and learning more about fish. Call ahead for details and reservations for your group.

DIRECTIONS: From Palatka, take SR 17 twenty miles south to CR 309. Turn right on CR 309 and follow it south six miles to the aquarium on the left (east) side of the road. The observation tower and production ponds are three miles further south on the left (east) side of the road.

Aquarium open 7:00 A.M. to 3:30 P.M.; observation tower open sunrise to sunset. Best months for birding are January–December.

(386) 467-2374.

28. Ocala National Forest: Salt Springs

DESCRIPTION: The Salt Springs site in the Ocala National Forest offers a trail through scrubby flatwoods down to a hardwood forest along the clear, cold spring run, as Floridians call a watercourse that runs from a spring. Enter at the spring entrance itself for quick access to the spring, or park and hike for free at the trailhead just south of the springs. The trail is scrubby, so you'll get some migrants in season, and at the water's edge look for waders and limpkins. Anytime you are driving in the Ocala National Forest, watch for scrub-jays on the wires when you're passing their optimum habitat—scrub oak brush about five feet tall. Red-cockaded woodpecker trees are marked with white painted bands and can be found in clusters throughout the forest. For information on specific sites, call the forest office at (352) 625-2520. Salt Springs is a popular swimming location and can get very busy, so birding is best in the mornings and on weekdays. There is hunting on this property— dates and times are available by calling the forest office.

DIRECTIONS: Salt Springs is located just north of the intersection of CR 314 and CR 19 on the northeast side of the Ocala National Forest. The hiking trailhead is about half a mile south of the Salt Springs campground entrance, on the east side of the road.

Trail open twenty-four hours a day. Best months for birding are October– April.

(352) 685-2048.

The Unexpected Economics of Birding

Julie A. Brashears

Until recently, there was an easy formula for attracting tourists to Florida: Pave it, prune it, tame it, air-condition it, and they will come. Only now, tourists and residents alike are driving a growing industry in search of what Florida once was and, in some of its last untouched corners, still is.

Nature-based tourism is on the rise, and birdwatchers make up one of its largest groups. Nationwide, birding is big business: 54 million Americans defined themselves as birdwatching enthusiasts in 1994. Florida is second in the nation (behind California) in the amount of retail sales generated by nonconsumptive bird use,[1] which supports more than thirteen thousand jobs.[2] Birders devote much time, effort, and money to their hobby, and they contribute significantly to local economies by spending money on everything from gasoline to hotel rooms. A 1993–94 study found that birding in the Corkscrew Swamp Sanctuary area of southwest Florida had an economic impact of $9.4 million on the local communities.[3] It is estimated that nonconsumptive bird use generates more than $477 million in retail sales in Florida every year.[4]

As you might imagine, the tourism industry is taking notice. Birders and other nature tourists are turning conventional wisdom on its ear: they prefer areas that are wild—in fact, the fewer capital improvements in an area, the more likely it is to attract birds and birders! In Texas, where a birding trail is already calling attention to the economic impact of birding, communities are clamoring for—and getting—birding tourists. They not only tailor their services to birders, but they are conserving their habitat and restoring damaged wildlands to attract birds and the birders that follow them.

Your birding dollars, when recognized as such, are a vote for conservation. They lobby local communities to conserve their resources, not only for the health of their environment but for the health of their economy.

Here are some simple ways you can use your economic might to motivate conservation:

(1) Always make sure you're recognizable as a nature tourist or birdwatcher. If you are not recognized as a nature tourist, you are assumed to be a traditional tourist, for whom communities will continue to pave and develop their wildlands. Every time you eat at a restaurant, buy gas, or stay in a hotel while on a birding trip, talk to people so that they recognize the growing proportion of their business that comes from birders. Compliment them on their healthy wildlands.

(2) Patronize "responsible" businesses and tell them why. Businesses that landscape with native plants, give back to local wildlands or restoration efforts, and provide educational opportunities for the local community should be rewarded with our economic support and praise.

(3) Don't fall prey to false "ecomarketing." As the size of the ecotourism market is gaining attention, more businesses want to share in the wealth. Be an educated consumer. Tell tour operators that you pay to see the natural behavior of animals, not their panicked reactions to disturbance. Tell them you don't want a canned experience—captive wildlife or wildlife lured by food—and that you recognize that a natural experience means you might not see your target species every time, but that doesn't diminish your having a good time. Lastly, patronize businesses that not only show you wildlife but teach you about that wildlife too.

Notes

1. *Bird Conservation* (Spring 1997).

2. "The 1996 Economic Benefits of Watchable Wildlife Recreation in Florida" (May 1998), Southwick Associates.

3. P. Kerlinger, "The Economic Impacts of Birding Ecotourism on the Corkscrew Swamp Sanctuary Area, Florida, 1993–1994," 1994.

4. *Bird Conservation* (Spring 1997).

Second Subsection Map

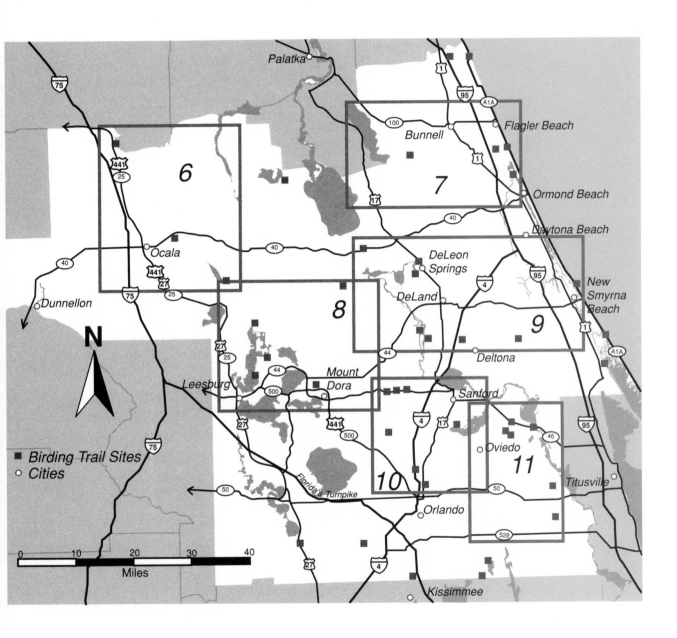

Limpkin Cluster

29. Sportsman's Cove   47

30. Silver River State Park   47

31. Ocklawaha Prairie Restoration Area   48

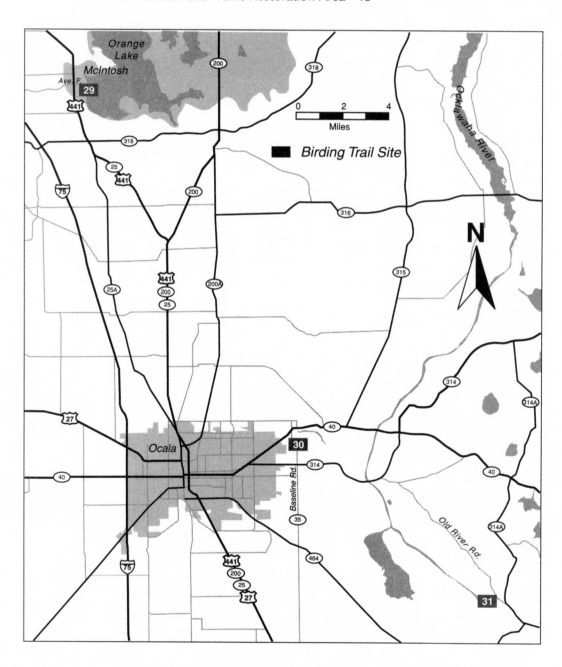

29. Sportsman's Cove

DESCRIPTION: Sportsman's Cove is a privately run fish camp on Orange Lake, a large lake known for its shorebird, wading bird, and wintering duck populations. From the waterfront you can scope for shorebirds on the flats. A reasonably priced nature tour by pontoon boat is also available. Lakes in this area are well known for their diversity in winter: shorebirds are thick here, and common loons, pied-billed and horned grebes, and even red phalaropes have been seen swimming in these lakes. Most important, this is the most likely site in the East Florida section of the Birding Trail to see a limpkin, year-round (barring drought conditions). Visit the waterfront in the morning and look for their leavings—the shells of mussels and snails. The birds are fairly habituated to human presence, so if you are patient and quiet, you're likely to get an excellent look at this amazing bird.

DIRECTIONS: From I-75 south of Gainesville, exit at CR 318 and drive east two and a half miles to US 441. Turn left (north) on US 441 and go three miles into the town of McIntosh. Turn right (east) on Avenue F. The site is eight blocks east of 441 at the end of Avenue F.

Open sunrise to sunset. Best months for birding are October–April.

(352) 591-1435.

30. Silver River State Park

DESCRIPTION: Silver River State Park encompasses a variety of habitats and is very accessible to the beginning birder. On the drive in, through scrub and sandhill habitats, watch for woodpeckers, turkeys, and bobwhite. At the end of the road, park in the lot by the barn. The Silver River Museum is open on weekends and interprets the natural history and paleontology of the area. Two trails begin in this general area. The nature trail leaves from the museum and loops down to the river and back, through oak hammock. Watch for migratory songbirds in season, and wading birds and limpkins down by the river. A second hiking trail, called the Swamp Trail, leaves from behind the barn and leads down, through a wetland and some pastures, to the river. Birding along the nature trail is better than the Swamp Trail, but the nature trail is also more heavily traveled. Bird walks are scheduled monthly, so call for details.

DIRECTIONS: Take SR 40 east from Ocala to SR 35 in Silver Springs. Turn right (south) on SR 35 (Baseline Road) and go approximately one mile to the state park entrance on the left (east) side of the road.

Open 8:00 A.M. to sunset. Best months for birding are October–April.

(352) 236-7148.

www.dep.state.fl.us/parks.

31. Ocklawaha Prairie Restoration Area

DESCRIPTION: The Ocklawaha Prairie property was acquired by the St. Johns River Water Management District to help in the restoration of the Ocklawaha's system of wetlands. Currently the site is an excellent spot for ducks, shorebirds, and wading birds, as wells as raptors, sparrows, and blackbirds. Park at the public parking site and hike the three-quarter-mile trail to the levee that parallels the wetland. An overlook at this point gives you a higher vantage of the marsh; bird along the levee trail, remembering it is not a loop and you will need to return the way you came. Portions of this property will be closed intermittently for the ongoing restoration of the area. The Water Management District has a unique arrangement with a concessionaire on the property called the Refuge at Ocklawaha. Guided birding trips for groups are available through this vendor, and the site has overnight accommodations as well. Call ahead for details and reservations.

DIRECTIONS: From Ocala, take SR 40 east fourteen miles to CR 314A. Turn right (south) on CR 314A and go seven miles. Turn right on Old River Road and follow it less than a mile to the public parking area.

Open sunrise to sunset. Best months for birding are October–April.

Refuge at Ocklawaha, (352) 288-2233.

http://sjr.state.fl.us/

Florida's Fabulous Waders

Susan D. Jewell

If we could lump the habitat needs of wading birds into a simple phrase, it would be "flat, wet, and warm." That describes most of Florida, and explains why the state is such a mecca for this group of long, tall birds—long legs, necks, and bills. Nineteen species of wading birds—egrets, herons, ibises, spoonbills, wood storks, limpkins, bitterns, night herons, and cranes—call Florida their home, more than any other state, and essentially have defined Florida bird life for a century. All may be seen in the East Florida section of the Great Florida Birding Trail.

Florida's generally flat terrain combined with high annual rainfalls encourages water to accumulate in marshes, swamps, ditches, and other depressions. Usually water remains at least a few days, if not months. These depressions may be temporarily inactive while dry, but the aquatic life that wading birds feed on returns amazingly fast with the addition of water. Crayfish, snails, and freshwater shrimp become active and quickly reproduce. Frogs and insects migrate in, and fish arrive as waterways reconnect. The broader the water coverage, the more the birds can disperse. During the dry season, generally December to April, with fewer and smaller watering holes available, the birds will concentrate and be easier for birders to spot.

Most wader species are found year-round in northeast Florida. Within a species, some individuals are residents and some migrate between Florida and the northern states or Canada. Great numbers of herons, egrets, and ibises arrive from northern states around November or December to spend the winter, returning north again around March. The ones that stay in Florida start nesting as early as January, but primarily in March or April. Thus the winter months, when both migrant and resident waders are present and concentrated around the remaining wetlands, are the best time to look for wading birds.

On stiltlike legs, these graceful birds wade through the shallow water, searching for small aquatic prey. Infinite patience and a lightning-quick jab with a razor-sharp bill usually bring a reward—a fish, a tadpole, a crayfish, or a shrimp. The calmer the water, the better the birds can see any movement of unlucky prey.

We can make many generalizations about wading bird species, but they each have some characteristic traits. Green herons, for example, with their relatively short legs, often perch on low branches over water to watch for prey. Wood storks, which have touch-sensitive bills, often feed at night. White ibises also have touch-sensitive bills that help them find crayfish in the mud. During the breeding season, most wading birds don showier plumes to attract mates. These plumes may be longer, softer, or more colorful, depending on the species. Among the showiest are the great and snowy egrets, with long, soft white plumes that drape well beyond the body plumage. These breeding plumes caused the demise of many species of Florida's wading birds during the late 1800s. Birds were shot so the plumes could adorn the hats of wealthy women. Most species have made significant recoveries in their populations, but none have returned to the numbers they enjoyed before the plume slaughters.

Because they are so dependent on standing water, changes in weather patterns may dictate where you'll find wading birds. They prefer feeding in fresh water but are often found in brackish or even salt water. If you are near a breeding colony or a nocturnal roost, the evening skies will be etched with the flight lines of wading birds winging their way back to rest for the night.

Warbler Hammocks Cluster

32. Haw Creek Preserve at Russell Landing   52

33. Bulow Creek State Park   52

34. North Peninsula State Park   53

35. Tomoka State Park   54

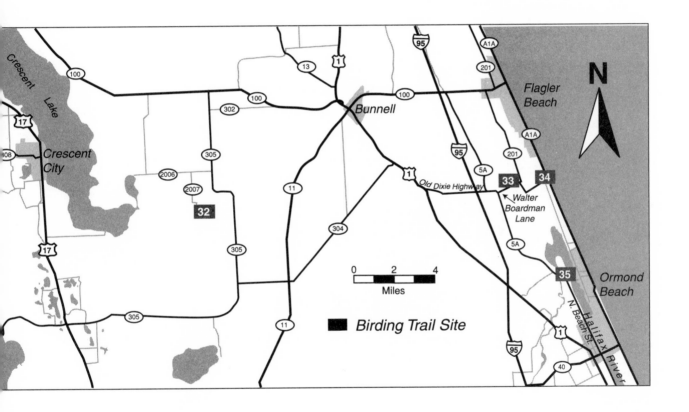

32. Haw Creek Preserve at Russell Landing

DESCRIPTION: Russell Landing's unique boardwalk elevates the birder for closer viewing of the canopy in this bottomland hardwood forest. Seasonal changes in rainfall mean the ground beneath the boardwalk can be dry or under water, changing the composition of species you'll see at each point. Woodpeckers and sapsuckers make this preserve their home year-round, and prothonotary warblers nest in the cypress margin of the creek. During migration, mixed flocks of warblers move through the property and swallow-tailed kites can be seen soaring overhead. Take one of the many boardwalk spurs to the blackwater Haw Creek to look for waders, including limpkin. The fallow field at the end of the boardwalk is good for sparrows and raptors. The roads leading to this site are rustic, but passable; four-wheel drive is unnecessary except in periods of extreme rain.

DIRECTIONS: From Bunnell, take SR 100 west six miles to CR 305. Turn left (south) and go three miles to CR 2006. Turn right (west) and go a mile and a half to CR 2007, a dirt road. Turn left (south) and go two miles to the park at the end. The road will dogleg left (east) before the park entrance.

Open sunrise to sunset. Best months for birding are October–April.

(386) 437-7490.

33. Bulow Creek State Park

DESCRIPTION: The beautiful Bulow Creek park features a shorebird mecca that fronts on Walter Boardman Lane. It is tempting to pull off the road here to scope for all the birds, but resist temptation! The road margin is very narrow and scoping for a lesser yellowlegs just isn't worth being clipped by a passing car. To remedy this situation, the Florida Park Service and local Audubon chapters installed an observation platform on this wetland, Boardman Pond, which can be accessed by parking at the entrance just west of the bridge and hiking north to the spur that leads to the overlook. Walk carefully to the end, to avoid flushing the birds, and scope for the diversity of shorebirds which has included avocets, dunlin, both yellowlegs, western sandpipers, and a variety of migratory ducks. This same trail leads north to the vaulted ceilings of the Bulow Plantation Ruins' ancient hammocks, and on the way overlooks Bulow Creek and its associated marshes. Wading birds and songbirds, raptors and creepers, this site's a great experience if you're willing to walk.

DIRECTIONS: From I-95 north of Ormond Beach, exit at Old Dixie Highway and drive east one mile. When the road curves south, Walter Boardman Lane branches off to the left (east). Turn east and go approximately half a mile to the entrance to Bulow Creek State Park. Look for a small parking area on the right (south) side of Boardman Lane, just beyond the wetland pond on the left, before (west of) the bridge over Bulow Creek.

Open 8:00 A.M. to sunset. Best months for birding are October–April.

(386) 676-4050.

www.dep.state.fl.us/parks.

34. North Peninsula State Park

DESCRIPTION: A beach park, North Peninsula is great for observing terns, gulls, shorebirds, and gannets; the property on the west side of A1A is home to several scrub-jay families. While driving A1A or Highbridge Road, watch the telephone lines and posts for Florida scrub-jays. The drive between Bulow Creek State Park and North Peninsula is very scenic with good wading birds also—travel Walter Boardman Lane east to Highbridge Road and continue east on Highbridge to get from Bulow to North Peninsula.

DIRECTIONS: North Peninsula State Park is located six miles south of Flagler Beach on SR A1A.

Open 8:00 A.M. to sunset. Best months for birding are January–December.

(386) 676-4050.

www.dep.state.fl.us/parks.

35. Tomoka State Park

DESCRIPTION: The Tomoka and Halifax Rivers border this peninsula park, offering a variety of birding experiences for a variety of interests and abilities. Birding can be done in the Tomoka hammock by car, if necessary, but is better on foot, particularly at Tomoka Point where warblers like black-throated blues and Cape Mays tend to gather during migration. From the boat basin and Tomoka Point, birders can scope the rivers for terns, pelicans, loons, and ducks, while bald eagles and swallow-tailed kites soar overhead. Canoe rentals are available from the boat basin to explore and bird the Tomoka River. Educational programs are available, as staffing permits, by appointment. Call in advance for details and reservations.

DIRECTIONS: From I-95, take SR 40 toward Ormond Beach. Drive east five miles to the light at the west approach to the Ormond Bridge over the Halifax River. Turn left (north) before the bridge onto North Beach Street and proceed four miles north to the entrance to Tomoka State Park.

Open 8:00 A.M. to sunset. Best months for birding are October–April.

(386) 676-4050.

www.dep.state.fl.us/parks.

Swallow-Tailed Kites

Masters of the Wind

Ken Meyer

The plane sliced the horizon diagonally as I scanned the mottled vegetation below my window for a glint of white. Like hidden faces that suddenly appear in a cloud, a few white specks in the distance suddenly materialized into birds. Seconds later, the few became hundreds—hundreds of swallow-tailed kites gliding through the south Florida sky, their bright white heads offset by black upper wings, blue-gray backs, and sharply forked tails.

From the airplane, we were following the radio signal of a juvenile kite that I had equipped, as a nestling, two months earlier, with a transmitter in Big Cypress National Preserve. Like its companions, on this morning the young bird was rising on thermals from a temporary communal night roost to forage and "kite" for food. The kite would acquire fat over the next few weeks, mainly from eating flying insects, to fuel its upcoming migration to South America, an imposing challenge for a bird that hatched just three months earlier in a nest at the top of slash pine.

With its striking black-and-white plumage, deeply forked tail, and extraordinary aerial grace, the swallow-tailed kite is rarely misidentified as it courses low over the treetops of Florida's spring runs, rivers, and other forested wetlands. Even from great distances, these kites can be distinguished from hawks and vultures by their silhouette, slightly down-curved wings, and tendency to hang motionless while heading upwind. They rarely flap their wings but almost continuously rotate their tails, often to nearly ninety degrees, in order to hold a heading, turn abruptly, or trace tight circles across the sky.

It is fitting that Florida plays a central role in the conservation of swallow-tailed kites. While their historic breeding range included parts of perhaps twenty-one states, extending up the Mississippi River drainage system as far north as Minnesota, their current range is limited to Florida and small parts of only six other states. Swallow-tails breed in the southeastern United States, but they migrate south in late summer, spending our winter months in South America. This bird's population suffered an abrupt decline at the turn of the twentieth century, perhaps as the result of shooting and habitat loss, and is presently estimated at 800 to 1,200 pairs in the United States, or a total of 3,500 to 5,000 birds at the end of each nesting season. Another subspecies nests from southern Mexico to central South America and is virtually unstudied.

Since 1996 we have undertaken a satellite tracking study of the United States population of kites to identify their migration corridor and wintering range, both of which were previously unknown. With this technology we have watched the southbound route of "tagged" kites unfold as they soared along a narrow path to Cuba, the Yucatan Peninsula, then down the eastern coastal plain of Central America and into Colombia, where they funneled through the Andes and hugged the southern fringe of the Amazon Basin before spilling into the region surrounding the Pantanal in southwestern Brazil, one of the world's largest and most spectacular wetland systems—in a journey of nearly five thousand miles over the leisurely span of three months.

Without question, the sight of hundreds of swallow-tailed kites serenely perched and preening, then swirling upward in the morning sun, as they do in late summer at premigration roosts around Florida, is compelling enough reason to pursue the conservation of natural lands in our state today. The vulnerability and endurance of this extraordinary bird make it a fitting emblem, as well, for the Great Florida Birding Trail.

Swallow-Tailed Kite Cluster

36. Ocala National Forest: Alexander Springs   58

37. Sunnyhill Restoration Area   58

38. Emeralda Marsh Conservation Area   59

39. Emeralda Marsh Conservation Area (Treasure Island Entrance)   59

40. Hidden Waters Preserve   60

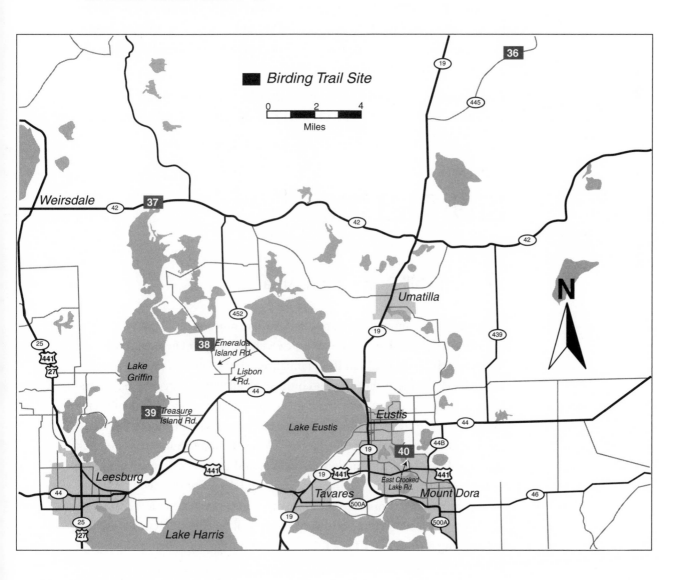

36. Ocala National Forest: Alexander Springs

DESCRIPTION: Alexander Springs in the Ocala National Forest offers a hardwood hammock along a clear, cold spring run, attractive to migratory songbirds in season. Swallow-tailed kites can be seen frequently, soaring over the run in the late spring and summer, and barred owls call to one another in the hammock. Take the Timucuan Trail from the beach area to access the hammock and two overlooks on the spring run. Watch the run for wading birds and limpkins. Anytime you are driving in the Ocala National Forest, watch for scrub-jays on the wires, and pull off when the road crosses rivers to check for limpkin. Red-cockaded woodpecker trees are marked with white painted bands and can be found in clusters throughout the forest. Alexander Springs is a popular swimming location and can get very busy; birding is best in the mornings and on weekdays.

DIRECTIONS: From SR 19 north of Eustis, take CR 445 northeast five miles. The entrance to Alexander Springs will be on the left (north) side of the road.

Open 8:00 A.M. to sunset. Best months for birding are October–May.

(352) 669-3153.

37. Sunnyhill Restoration Area

DESCRIPTION: Sunnyhill Restoration Area has miles of trails and levees for exploring the marshland of the historic Ocklawaha River channel. Follow the levees, watching for ducks in the channelized river—blue-winged and green-winged teal, northern shoveler, and bufflehead all winter here, among others. Wading birds including glossy and white ibis are common, and purple gallinule and least bittern nest here. Swallows and martins love the open areas and channel and can be seen feeding en masse over the water. Songbirds are thick through the area, as are turkeys, bobwhite, and a variety of sparrows. Take water and a hat in warm weather: the trails and dikes are exposed to full sun. Access the property from the Blue House parking area and check the kiosk for a map of the area. Portions of this property will be closed intermittently for the ongoing restoration. Check for closures at the entrance before birding the property.

Directions: From Weirsdale, take CR 42 east 5.9 miles. The Blue House entrance to Sunnyhill is on the left (north) side of the road.

Open sunrise to sunset. Best months for birding are September–May.

http://sjr.state.fl.us.

38 and 39. Emeralda Marsh Conservation Area

Description: The large Emeralda Marsh Conservation Area on Lake Griffin offers a diversity of birding opportunities with so many miles of dike trails that you could spend all day hiking this property alone. Check the Treasure Island entrance for raptors, shorebirds, wading birds, and migratory songbirds. The main entrances along Emeralda Island Road are currently open and also have good sparrow habitat and host large flocks of bobolinks each spring. Least and American bitterns are prolific, and migratory ducks frequent the impoundments in the fall and winter. Mottled ducks can be found here year-round. Check at any entrance kiosk for a map of the property or download one off the website before you go. There is seasonal duck hunting, so call ahead for seasons if you wish. The ongoing restoration of this property means portions will be closed intermittently. A new wildlife drive will be open some weekends. For details, contact the Lake County Visitor Center at (352) 429-3673.

Directions: From Leesburg, take US 441 northeast two miles to CR 44. For the Treasure Island access, turn northwest on Treasure Island Road and, at the four-way stop, proceed on North Treasure Island Avenue to the site at the end. For the main property, take CR 44 to Lisbon Road and turn left (north). When the road comes to a T, turn left and follow Emeralda Island Road northwest. Accesses to the marsh property will be on both sides, with occasional closures for this area's ongoing restoration.

Open sunrise to sunset. Best months for birding are October–May.

For hunt information, (386) 329-4404.

http://sjr.state.fl.us.

40. Hidden Waters Preserve

DESCRIPTION: Hidden Waters is worth a visit if you are already in the Eustis–Mount Dora area. The property has remarkable topography for Florida—a rapid change in elevation of more than a hundred feet makes this an interesting destination. Steep, sloping sides lead to a sinkhole formed over time by underground water sources. The hardwood forest that surrounds the lake can be productive for songbirds in season. Recorded birds include redstarts, black-throated blue warblers, and great crested flycatchers in early October and again in early April. The open, fallow areas are good for raptors, and the elusive Cooper's hawk has been seen on the property. Check the lake for ducks and wading birds.

DIRECTIONS: From the intersection of SR 44B and US 441 in Mount Dora, take US 441N west 0.8 miles. Turn right (north) at East Crooked Lake Road and go 0.4 miles to Country Club Road. Turn right on Country Club and go 0.7 miles. Park entrance is on the right.

Open sunrise to sunset. Best months for birding are March–April, October–November.

(352) 343-3777.

www.lcwa.org.

Bird Migration

A Biannual Stretching of the Wings

Jim Cox

Migration was one of the first natural phenomena our ancestors ever noticed. Consider this question posed in the Book of Job (39:26) a few thousand years ago: "Doth the hawk fly by thy wisdom and stretch her wings toward the south?"

In Florida, birding reaches fever pitch during migration. About a quarter of the songbirds recorded in Florida pass through only during migration, in a biannual "stretching of the wings" that provides the only chance to see some of our most colorful songbirds. The timing of migration in Florida depends upon the bird. Louisiana waterthrushes begin their fall migration in late July; bay-breasted warblers don't move through until early October. Purple martins, one of the earliest spring migrants, arrive in late January, while migratory cuckoos can be seen into early June. The peak period in fall for most songbirds lies between mid-September and mid-October. In spring the peak is mid-April, though good numbers can be seen from mid-March into early May.

Weather plays a key role, since birds like to move with favorable tailwinds and clear skies. You can usually find some migrants anytime in the proper seasons, but bigger numbers will come your way in response to the weather. In fall, go birding as cold fronts approach, and a day or so just after they pass. There will be a noticeable scarcity of birds as you move your birding time farther away from a passing front, which provides the birds with strong tailwinds. The best spring trips generally occur just after a cold front passes west to east across the state in April; it meets the birds heading north and causes them to "fall out," particularly in coastal areas.

Change is the rule during migration, and each trip afield is unique, as variation in the individual timing and weather lead to a daily reshuffling of the birds. Many songbirds reach their wintering grounds by traveling in a series of long-distance "leaps" interspersed with days of resting and refueling. The long flights are initiated at night; birds leave just after dark and travel well past midnight. On full-moon nights in September and October, you can observe this phenomenon by training your binoculars on the moon. Occasionally you will see a shadowy figure shoot across—a migratory songbird heading toward balmy climates further south.

Songbirds may seem like slim and trim creatures, but migration is a process fueled by fat. Birds concentrate energy by increasing their fat content tenfold during their refueling stops (while also often doubling their weight). The fat energy that a blackpoll warbler uses as it crosses the Gulf of Mexico is equal to the energy a human would use if it ran four-minute miles nonstop for eighty hours. If the blackpoll warbler were burning gasoline instead of body fat, it could boast of getting 720,000 miles to the gallon!

Why birds migrate is still something of a mystery. Most theories hold that migration enables birds to utilize seasonally abundant resources, like the bugs in a northern bog, while living in favorable climates during other times of the year. Songbirds that winter in the tropics generally survive better than songbirds that remain in cooler areas of North America.

Whatever the reason and whatever the means, migration is a time to get out and enjoy the seasonal "stretching of the wings." The colors are great, the numbers daunting, the mechanics utterly mesmerizing, and we get a chance to bid "safe travels" to the animals that fill our world with music and color.

The Scrub and the Scrub-Jay

Imperiled Natural Treasures of Florida

Reed Bowman and Glen Woolfenden

Florida scrub-jays make it easy to be a birdwatcher. Their blue-and-gray plumage is pleasing, they live in a very specific habitat, and they like to sit on exposed perches. Go to their identified haunts and they'll be easy to spot.

Unlike its cousin the common blue jay, which ranges over a large portion of the United States, the Florida scrub-jay is restricted to Florida, the only bird so distinguished. That's because scrub-jays can live in only one habitat—low-growing, open oak scrubs, occurring on the well-drained sandy ridges of central Florida. Oak scrubs support a varied community of plants and animals, and some, like the scrub-jay, are found nowhere else in the world.

Unfortunately the jay's favorite haunts, open oak scrubs, are fast disappearing. And as its habitat is destroyed, so goes the jay: less than 10 percent of the large population of scrub-jays that once lived in the state still survives.

Scrub-jays prefer scrubs where the oaks are only one to three meters tall and are interspersed with open patches of bare sand. This habitat structure is maintained by frequent fires, ignited by lightning during summer thunderstorms. Without fire, oak scrubs become pine forests with tall, dense oak understories, causing scrub-jays and many other species endemic to oak scrubs to disappear. Frequent fires, perhaps once every ten to twenty years, are natural and regenerate habitat, not only for scrub-jays but for the entire scrub community.

Florida scrub-jays differ greatly from their closest relatives, the scrub-jays of western North America, because of the unique habitat they occupy, and because of their rare social system of cooperative breeding wherein young jays from the previous breeding season become "helpers" and assist their parents with sibling care, predator control, and territory defense. When the family group is foraging, one jay usually stands sentinel, watching for and alerting the other group members to potential predators. This behavior is effective only in open habitat—hence the jays' preference for low-growing, open scrub.

Although jays are true opportunists when feeding—for example, a big snake is a potential predator, but a small snake is a meal—they rely on insects and acorns for the bulk of their diet. During the fall, each jay harvests and caches more than six thousand acorns, a good third of which it recovers and eats throughout the winter.

Florida's scrub-jay population has declined because of dramatic habitat loss, habitat modification, mostly from fire suppression, and habitat fragmentation. Remaining scrub patches are becoming smaller and farther apart. As the habitats between patches are converted to cities, groves, or pine plantations, the probability that jays can move between scrub patches plummets.

Despite drastic declines throughout recent decades, the recipe for conserving jays has but a few ingredients. Identify the remnant scrubs and preserve them. If they are overgrown and no longer suitable for jays, we can restore them through the introduction of fire. As long as scrub is burned frequently, it can be maintained as optimal scrub-jay habitat. So, the prescription for conserving scrub and its unique fauna and flora is simple: Purchase scrub and manage it. The Florida scrub-jay can and should be a symbol of successful conservation. Preserve this jay and we preserve an entire community of rare and unique species.

Scrub-Jay Cluster

41. Lake George State Forest   66

42. DeLeon Springs State Park   66

43. Lake Woodruff National Wildlife Refuge   67

44. Hontoon Island State Park   68

45. Blue Spring State Park   68

46. Lyonia Preserve   69

47. Lake Ashby Park   70

48. Smyrna Dunes Park   71

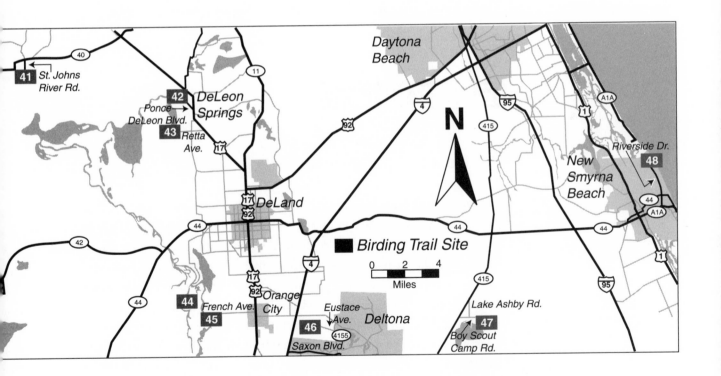

41. Lake George State Forest

DESCRIPTION: Lake George State Forest could be a quick stop or a long hike: drive to the end of the road into Bluffton Recreation Area and decide for yourself. Along the way, you may see eagles, turkeys, bobwhite, and raptors, as well as songbird migrants in a thick hardwood hammock, swallow-tailed kites, and limpkins and other wading birds at the end access to the St. Johns River. If the birds are there, it's worth hiking the property more extensively to see what kind of migrants you can turn up. Occasionally this property is closed for hunting, so check the entrance kiosk for dates, or call ahead.

DIRECTIONS: The site is located just east of the town of Volusia on the St. Johns River. Take SR 40 east half a mile to St. Johns River Road and turn right (south). Go three-quarters of a mile to the forest entrance gate. The drive to the river extends two and one-half miles further south on St. Johns River Road.

Open sunrise to sunset. Best months for birding are January–December.

(386) 985-7822.

www.fl-dof.com.

42. DeLeon Springs State Park

DESCRIPTION: Located just north of Lake Woodruff National Wildlife Refuge, the spring run from DeLeon Springs State Park flows into Lake Woodruff. Check the waterfront here for coots, ducks, and limpkins and other wading birds, then hike the five-mile trail through hydric hammock and a boardwalk across floodplain forest and cypress margin, looking for hermit thrushes and blue-winged warblers, redstarts and cerulean warblers among others during migration. A concessionaire-run boat tour leaves from the recreation area's dock and takes trips down to Lake Woodruff, an excellent way to see bald eagles, swallow-tailed kites, and myriad species of wintering ducks on the national wildlife refuge's lake.

DIRECTIONS: From I-4, exit north on US 17/92. Choose US 17 north to DeLeon Springs, and turn left (west) on the north side of town onto Ponce DeLeon Boulevard. Cross the railroad tracks; the road ends at the park.

Open 8:00 A.M. to sunset. Best months for birding January–April, October–December.

(386) 985-4212.

www.dep.state.fl.us/parks.

43. Lake Woodruff National Wildlife Refuge

DESCRIPTION: This series of impoundments provides important resting and feeding areas for waterfowl, wading birds, and shorebirds, especially in winter. Trails follow the dikes around a series of pools of varying depths in which you can see yellowlegs, fulvous whistling ducks, short-billed dowitchers, and American bitterns. Pick up a map at the entrance, and hike especially to the tower overlook constructed by West Volusia Audubon at the intersection of the three pools. A fixed scope at the top helps you to scour the pools for ducks in the vegetation and watch the tree line for raptors scanning for a meal. Nature trails south of the entrance area offer hammocks good for songbird migrants, as do the flatwoods on the northwest side of the impoundments. The refuge staff and the local Audubon chapter offer nature programs and, once a year, a driving tour of the dikes. Call ahead for the schedule or stop in at the refuge office during your visit.

DIRECTIONS: From US 17 north of DeLand, turn west on Retta Street and drive to Grand Avenue. Turn left (south) and proceed to Mud Lake Road. Turn right (west) and drive to the refuge entrance at the end of Mud Lake Road.

Open sunrise to sunset. Best months for birding are January–April, October–December.

(386) 985-4673.

44. Hontoon Island State Park

DESCRIPTION: To access Hontoon Island State Park, leave your car and take the free ferry across the narrow stretch of river to the other side, where you can immediately bird for osprey, anhingas, and limpkins and other wading birds along the water's edge. Pick up a map of the area and plot your course: the hiking trail down the western side of the island leads through hardwood hammocks full of songbirds and woodpeckers, and ends at an ancient Native American midden two miles later. Swallow-tailed kites and bald eagles circle over the hammock and you can make out their forms beyond the sun-dappled leaf canopy. The interior of the island is comprised of scrubby flatwoods good for warblers and vireos. Of note, the island has comfortable, affordable camp cabins for rent, which allow you access to the island at night and early in the morning.

DIRECTIONS: From DeLand, take SR 44 west to Old New York Avenue. Turn left and go approximately two and a half miles to Hontoon Road. Turn left and travel one mile to River Ridge Road. Turn left and the parking area will be two miles ahead on the left side of the road.

Open 8:00 A.M. to sunset. Best months for birding are January–May, September–December.

(386) 736-5309.

www.dep.state.fl.us/parks.

45. Blue Spring State Park

DESCRIPTION: Blue Spring is best known for the manatees that overwinter in its warm-water springs, but the habitats on the surrounding lands are excellent for birding too. Walk the spring run boardwalk looking for coots, anhingas, and cormorants in the water, and barred owls and migrating warblers in the oaks. A hiking trail leads off from the last parking area and winds for four miles past sand pine scrub, pine flatwoods, and freshwater marsh. This trail is a popular songbird hangout during migrations—but arrive early, and visit on weekdays, if possible. The park reaches capacity quickly with swimmers and manatee viewers, and once full, the park has to turn away other visitors. Guided tours are available for groups by calling in advance for details and reservations.

DIRECTIONS: From US 17/92 in Orange City, take French Avenue west two and a half miles to the park entrance just beyond the railroad crossing.

Open 8:00 A.M. to sunset. Best months for birding are March–April, October–December.

(386) 775-3663

www.dep.state.fl.us/parks

46. Lyonia Preserve

DESCRIPTION: Two syllables describe Lyonia: "scrub-jays." This preserve north of Deltona has many families of Florida scrub-jays inhabiting it, in part because the habitat is good for them, and in part because neighboring parcels of appropriate scrub are being gobbled up by development, as in much of Florida. If you hike the trails from behind the library before 10:00 A.M. and are patient and observant, there is a very high chance you will see this Florida specialty. Highly intelligent and very social, they have learned to take food from humans in some places. PLEASE DO NOT FEED SCRUB-JAYS. Not only can feeding these birds harm them by destroying their healthy wariness of humans, but the nutritionally inadequate foods we give them can harm the birds and the development of their young. In addition to jays, this property hosts other scrub specialties like white-eyed vireos, eastern towhees, and nighthawks. The pinelands on the south side of the property are home to red-headed woodpeckers and have a seasonal wetland at the center which harbors wading birds and ducks. Educational programs are available to groups; call in advance for details and reservations.

DIRECTIONS: From I-4 north of Deltona, take SR 472 east 2.7 miles to Providence Boulevard (CR 4155). Turn right (south), drive 0.7 miles to Eustace Avenue, and turn right (west). The library will be immediately on the left (south) side of the road. Park in the library's lot. The trailhead is located behind the library.

Open 6:00 A.M. to 8:00 P.M. Best months for birding are January–December.

(386) 740-5261.

www.volusia.org/growth/landacq.

47. Lake Ashby Park

DESCRIPTION: Birding the county park at Lake Ashby begins with the drive in. Watch for wood storks circling on thermals and turkeys under the oaks in the adjacent pastures. The flatwoods on the drive down the entrance road are good for vireos and pine warblers. At the parking area, leave your car and head down the trail that starts from the southeast side of the parking lot. The oak hammock gets wetter with each step you take, sloping down to the lake, and songbird migration makes for great birding if you have the birding-by-ear skills to identify the birds calling up in the canopy. At the end of the trail there is a boardwalk that loops through the lake cypress margin—watch for nesting prothonotary warblers in spring—and leads out over open water before returning to shore on the other side of a cove. Use this vantage to look for osprey and eagles soaring, waders at the lake edge, and terns plunging in the lake's center. An extended horse trail is open to the public and leads off to the west side of the property; this is worth hiking on productive migration days. Please respect adjacent private property owners by not crossing fence lines. The park can get busy on weekends with anglers and other users, so plan accordingly.

DIRECTIONS: From SR 44 east of Deland, take SR 415 south to Lake Ashby Road. Turn left and follow Lake Ashby Road to Boy Scout Camp Road. Turn left here and drive about one mile. The park entrance will be on the right (south) side of the road.

Open sunrise to sunset. Best months for birding are January–April, October–December.

(386) 428-4589.

48. Smyrna Dunes Park

DESCRIPTION: Smyrna Dunes is a county park on the south side of Ponce de Leon Inlet. Two miles of boardwalk wind around the perimeter. Moving counterclockwise from the parking lot, the trail first passes through some hammock good for warbler landfalls in spring migration, then on to the oceanfront where birders can check the beach for loafing gulls, terns, and shorebirds and scope the water for loons and ducks. Plovers like the north end of the beach by the inlet, and gannets sometimes plunge in the inlet's mouth. Wrapping around the west side of the point, boardwalk spurs lead out into the river, where you can scan sandbars for loafing shorebirds, pelicans and cormorants. On this easy two-mile walk you can spot a diversity of birds without ever leaving the boardwalk. Plan for the trail being exposed to full sun. Morning hours and low tide tend to be best for birding.

DIRECTIONS: In New Smyrna Beach, take SR 44 business straight (east) onto Canal Street. Turn left (north) onto Riverside Drive and then right onto Flagler Avenue, crossing the Halifax River to the barrier island. Upon reaching the other side, turn left (north) onto North Peninsula Drive. The park is at the end of the road, two miles ahead.

Open sunrise to sunset. Best months for birding are January–December.

(904) 424-2935.

www.volusia.org/parks/smyrnadunes.htm.

Birdwatching 101

The Tools of the Trade

Jim Cox

In contrast to the challenge of identifying confusing fall warblers, one of the easiest aspects of birdwatching is deciding how much equipment you need. The answer is, quite simply, "not much." There are only two essentials—binoculars and a field guide—and this certainly makes birding one of the least expensive hobbies a person can undertake. There are no rackets to string, no balls to lose, no nets to tie up, and no golf clubs or running shoes to buy. Perfectly adequate binoculars run anywhere from seventy to a hundred dollars, and a good field guide costs a pittance. Armed with these, you are well on your way.

Binoculars

As birding maven Peter Dunn has noted, "Binoculars are the instruments that define birding—the functional equivalent of the first baseman's glove, the musician's instrument, the plow in the hands of the frontier farmer." Good binoculars make for good birding, while bad binoculars lead to missed opportunities and splitting headaches induced by blurred images, double vision, and eyestrain.

Binoculars come in many different shapes and forms and carry such descriptions as "roof prism," "close focus," and "armor coated." At the outset you don't need to spend too much time deciphering this arcane lexicon. If you really get hooked on bird watching, you can learn more about binoculars later and trade in for better ones. I began with a thirty-dollar pair in 1976, and these were still performing fine until I decided I wanted to move up to higher-quality "glasses."

The proper pair of binoculars must give you a good field of view, focus quickly, fit your hands, withstand rain and fog, still come up swinging after an unintended fall to the ground, and enable you to see birds close at hand as well as across the field. Here are a few simple points to consider when purchasing your first pair.

First, make sure the power, or magnification, is at least 7–power. The power is the first number given in the numerical shorthand used to describe binoculars. A "7x35" pair of binoculars makes objects appear as if they are seven times as close as they actually are. Seven-power binoculars are about the minimum needed to see birds properly.

Second, try to make sure the second number (35 for a "7x35" pair of glasses) is at least five times as large as the power—for example, "7x35" or "8x40." This second number represents the diameter, in millimeters, of the large lens at the front of the binoculars (the "objective" lens or aperture). The larger this lens, the greater the amount of light the binoculars gather and thus the easier it will be to see characteristics in dim light or on a dull-colored bird.

Third, if you hold the binoculars about a foot away and look at the large lenses on the front, do they reflect a bluish or purplish tinge? This color is a special coating that is used to reduce the internal glare. If no coating is evident, the binoculars may produce a lower-quality image because the glare in the binoculars decreases the light that gets to your eyes.

Other questions to consider fall more into the realm of personal taste. Are the binoculars light enough to be carried for a couple of hours straight? Can you flex the barrels of the binoculars fairly easily and adjust them to the width of your eyes? If you wear glasses, do the rubber cups on the eyepieces fold back so you can use your glasses with the binoculars? When you look at a sign with large lettering, do the letters close to the edge of the field of view appear as precise and well-formed as the letters in the center of the field of view?

Optics for Birding (www.optics4birding.com) and A Better View Desired (www.lightshedder.com/BVD) are Internet websites that have up-to-date information and reviews of lots of optical equipment.

Field Guides

There has been a veritable explosion in the number of field guides published for birds over the last few years. Until the late 1960s, the guide most widely used was Roger Tory Peterson's *The Birds of Eastern North America,* the first field guide of its kind produced. This book made birding a popular activity by showing, clearly and concisely, the birds of woodlots and fields. Today, however, there are field guides available for certain regions of the country as well as for specific groups of birds. These specialized books may eventually make their way into the library of a birding enthusiast, but most experienced birders, and certainly all beginning birders, need only take a single, easy-to-carry, comprehensive field guide when they venture afield.

Four field guides have been especially popular over the last ten years and are considered to be the easiest for the beginning birdwatcher to use.

First, there's Roger Tory Peterson's *A Guide to the Birds of the Eastern United States, Second Edition,* available in most bookstores. Pictures in the Peterson guide have a clarity and consistency that are hard to find elsewhere, and this can be especially important to beginning birders. In addition the guide is limited to birds found in the eastern United States, which means that birders in Florida do not have to sort through multitudes of birds that do not occur here very often. Peterson also uses a simple, effective method of highlighting the distinguishing features of different species: he draws a line to the key identification features, visual cues that can save valuable time in the field. A bird could fly to the next county in the time it takes to read some of the descriptions provided in field guides.

The field guide that I cut my teeth on was *Birds of North America: A Guide to Field Identification,* by Chandler S. Robbins, Bertel Bruun, and Herbert S. Zim. Unlike the Peterson guide, this book deals with all the species that occur in North America, so you may spend some time flipping through pages of birds that aren't likely to occur in Florida. On the other hand, you won't need a second field guide if you take a trip to Colorado.

Another popular field guide for beginners is the National Geographic Society *Field Guide to the Birds of North America*. This book covers all birds north of Mexico and gives very good descriptions of the variation that certain birds exhibit in their color patterning. For example, red-shouldered hawks in Florida generally are a lighter color than red-shouldered hawks in other parts of the country. Most field guides mention this, but pictures in the National Geographic guide actually show this type of variation.

Finally, the *Stokes Field Guide to Birds: Eastern Region* has taken a new approach to bird identification. This guide uses some 940 color photographs rather than color paintings, and although photographs can prove tricky owing to variation in lighting conditions, background, and so on, the series of photographs presented here are generally very good.

Once you have selected your field guide, do not—repeat, do not—run off immediately looking for birds, because what you'll actually find instead could be trouble and frustration. Many a field guide has spent more time collecting dust than identifying birds because the owner didn't learn how to use the guide. Sit down with your new field guide and read through the complete introduction. Next, look at some of the pictures and figure out where some of the common birds you recognize are located in the field guide—front, back, or middle. Learning the organization of your guide is critical to using the book effectively, and the few hours you spending sitting in a chair will save you many more hours in the field.

There are other equipment issues in the world of birding—spotting scopes, magazines, bird recordings—but one final suggestion is worth mentioning here. Learning to identify birds by their songs may seem mystifying to the beginner, but it really doesn't require a musician's ear if you take a systematic approach and are willing to work at it (see page 110).

Tanager Cluster

49. Rock Springs Run State Reserve 77

50. Seminole State Forest 77

51. Lower Wekiva River Preserve State Park 78

52. Wekiwa Springs State Park 79

53. Lake Jesup Wilderness Area 79

54. Audubon Center for Birds of Prey 80

55. Mead Gardens 81

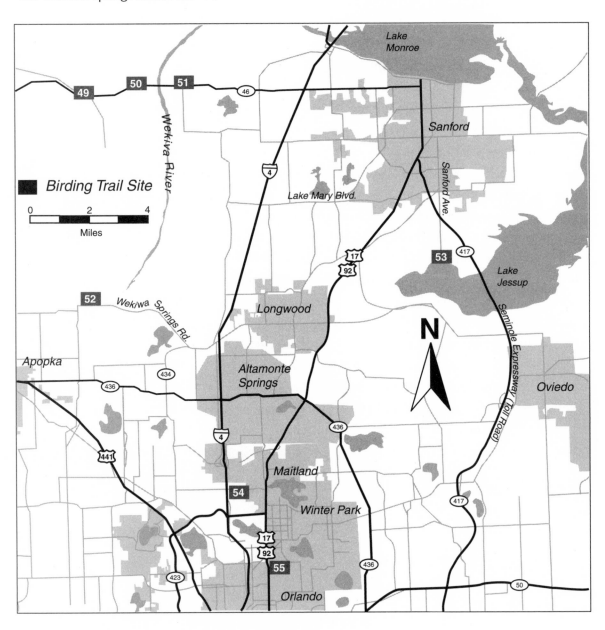

49. Rock Springs Run State Reserve

DESCRIPTION: The wild Rock Springs Run Reserve yields a good list of migratory songbirds if you take the time to hike its trails. Sandhill, hammock, and wetland species are present, as is the sought-after Florida scrub-jay. For this Florida native, drive the entrance road to the end of the pavement. Park and walk a bit down the dirt road addition and scrub-jays should be nearby. The best time for scrub-jay viewing is in the morning; these curious birds will generally post a sentinel atop a post or scrub oak to watch you pass.

DIRECTIONS: From I-4 north of Orlando, take SR 46 west 5.8 miles. The entrance road is on the left (south) side of the road.

Open 8:00 A.M. to 6:00 P.M. Best months for birding are October–April.

(407) 884-2008.

www.dep.state.fl.us/parks/district3/rocksprings.

50. Seminole State Forest

DESCRIPTION: Seminole State Forest is another large tract of wildlands in the Wekiva River Basin in which you could gladly lose yourself. More than 21,000 acres of scrub, sandhills, hammocks, and seasonal ponds, this property has hidden springs and the winding Blackwater Creek. Driving in is recommended to quickly access the best parts of the property; permits to drive in partway are obtained by calling in advance. Drive in and check the East Spur's scrub areas for Florida scrub-jays. Then continue to the bridge over Blackwater Creek. Watch for songbirds and limpkin along the creek, and hike along the Sulphur Loop or grade road watching for indigo buntings, vireos, and warblers galore, and listening to the laughter of pileated woodpeckers echoing through the wet palm hammocks. Canoes can be launched from the Blackwater Creek bridge; birding from the creek offers an alternative to hiking. Bring water and pick up a map before exploring this large tract. The southern and middle portions of the property offer better birding than the northern edges. There are seasonal hunts on this property. Call in advance for dates and closures.

DIRECTIONS: From I-4 north of Orlando, take SR 46 west five miles. The forest entrance is 2,000 feet west of the Wekiva River on the right (north) side of the road.

Open sunrise to sunset. Best months for birding are October–April.

(352) 360-6677.

www.fl-dof.com.

51. Lower Wekiva River Preserve State Park

DESCRIPTION: To bird the Lower Wekiva River Preserve, you can take a little time or a lot. The preserve encompasses more than 17,800 acres. You can hike the main trail north for miles through sandhills and flatwoods, or choose the one-mile self-guided sandhill nature trail. On the nature trail, expect birds like summer tanagers, Bachman's sparrows, yellow-throated warblers, eastern bluebirds, and brown-headed nuthatches. On the extended trail, everything from bobwhite to black-and-white warblers is a possibility. For the trail, take water and a map, remembering the trail does not loop, so you have to return the way you came.

DIRECTIONS: From I-4 north of Orlando, take SR 46 west 3.8 miles. The entrance to the property is on the right (north) side of the road.

Open sunrise to sunset. Best months for birding are October–April.

(407) 884-2008.

www.dep.state.fl.us/parks.

52. Wekiwa Springs State Park

DESCRIPTION: Wekiwa Springs is best known for its spring run, but it also includes some excellent habitats for birdwatching. The trail from the main spring to Sand Lake runs through six different plant communities, and in migration the park hosts thirty-four warbler species. Watch for red-headed, pileated, red-bellied, hairy, and downy woodpeckers; also, Bachman's sparrows are frequently heard calling in the sandhills. Canoe rentals are available from the spring, and the river offers wonderful birding opportunities, from prothonotary warblers to limpkins.

DIRECTIONS: From I-4 north of Orlando, take SR 434 west 0.9 miles to Wekiwa Springs Road. Turn right and go 4.1 miles to the park entrance.

Open 8:00 A.M. to sunset. Best months for birding are January–December.

(407) 884-2008.

www.dep.state.fl.us/parks.

53. Lake Jesup Wilderness Area

DESCRIPTION: This property in the Seminole County Natural Lands program is adjacent to a county boat launch on Lake Jesup. Bird the boat launch area for bald eagles, terns, wading birds, and white pelicans on the lake in winter. Then pick up a map of the wilderness area at the entrance kiosk in the hammock behind the boat ramp. A great horned owl likes this hammock at the entrance, so keep your eyes peeled. Hike in through the open pastureland, watching for raptors and sparrows. At the trail T, veer right and follow the berm trail to the hydric hammock at the end where you can watch for migratory songbirds in fall and spring and for resident barred owls year-round. Osprey, wading birds, and bald eagles all nest in the area, so watch for flyovers. This site is low-lying and naturally floods with seasonal fluctuations in the water level of Lake Jesup. Trails may be underwater at times, so be prepared to get your feet wet, especially in the summer rainy season.

DIRECTIONS: From Orlando, take I-4 north/east to Lake Mary Boulevard. Follow Lake Mary Boulevard east 5.5 miles to Sanford Avenue. Turn right (south) and follow it to the end at Lake Jesup Park.

Open sunrise to sunset. Best months for birding are October–April.

(407) 665-7352.

www.co.seminole.fl.us/natland/jesup.htm.

54. Audubon Center for Birds of Prey

DESCRIPTION: The Audubon Center for Birds of Prey has long been a rehabilitation facility for injured raptors. At least nineteen captive raptor species can be viewed daily at the center, including the bald eagle, peregrine falcon, Mississippi kite, Cooper's hawk, burrowing owl, great horned owl, crested caracara, and short-tailed hawk. The center's strong educational offerings include in-depth coverage of rehabilitation techniques, raptor biology, and identification, excellent for adults and children alike. If traveling in a group, call ahead to schedule a program.

DIRECTIONS: Exit I-4 at Lee Road on the north side of Orlando. Take Lee Road east to the first light, at Wymore Road, and turn left (north). At the first traffic light, turn right (east) on Kennedy Boulevard. Proceed 0.6 miles to East Avenue and turn left (north). At the stop sign, at Audubon Way, turn left into the parking lot.

Open Tuesday through Sunday, 10:00 A.M. to 4:00 P.M. Best months for birding are January–December.

(407) 644-0190.

www.adoptabird.org.

55. Mead Gardens

DESCRIPTION: Mead Gardens, a pocket of green amidst urban/suburban Orlando and Winter Park, is a haven for songbirds during migrations. In this city park, in September and October and again in April, a morning birding excursion can reap a list of fifteen or more warbler species, thrushes, redstarts, vireos, and kinglets, to name a few. Bird the boardwalk through the ephemeral wetland and also check the wooded edge along the stream and pond. The pond is home to wood ducks and may also host some waders. The oaks in the picnic area can be a good spot for gnatcatchers, kinglets, and vireos too. Weekends at the park can get busy, so bird early if you go on Saturday or Sunday.

DIRECTIONS: From I-4 north of downtown Orlando, take Fairbanks Avenue (SR 426) east toward Winter Park to Denning Drive. Turn right (south) and go half a mile to Garden Drive. Turn left (east). Mead Gardens is at the end of the road.

Open sunrise to sunset. Best months for birding are March–May, September–December.

(407) 599-3334.

www.ci.winter-park.fl.us.

A Beach in the Sky

Jeff Gore

I followed the manager down the aisles of Wal-Mart to the back of the store, through doors marked "Employees Only," and up a metal staircase to a dim, box-filled attic. She directed me between bicycles and Barbie dolls to a ladder that led to a locked hatch in the ceiling. I climbed the ladder, cracked open the hatch, and peered out onto a bright, sunlit roof covered with light brown gravel. There seemed to be acres of this flat gravel expanse, and except for the air-conditioners, it resembled nothing so much as an open stretch of beach. Clearly I wasn't the only one aware of the similarity: scattered across the roof were more than a hundred least terns and black skimmers incubating their eggs on the gravel, just as they typically do in nests scraped into flat, sandy areas along real Florida beaches.

Remarkably, this wasn't an unusual sight. I have seen exactly the same phenomenon on dozens of buildings throughout Florida—on hospitals, malls, condos, supermarkets, schools, and just about any other kind of building with a flat, gravel-covered roof. Although least terns and black skimmers are by far the most common rooftop residents, I've also encountered gull-billed terns, roseate terns, killdeer, and American oystercatchers nesting on roofs.

Why are these wild birds raising their young on rooftops? Most of these species also nest along relatively secluded beaches where their camouflaged eggs and colonial behavior offer defense against predators. But, as you can imagine, these ground-nesting birds are easily disturbed by beachgoers and their pets, and they can't nest on land that's been covered by concrete. It is tempting to conclude that birds have moved to roofs because we have driven them, one way or another, from suitable nesting sites on the beaches. That may well be, but it's also possible, human aesthetics notwithstanding, that birds have switched to roofs because they are a more desirable place to nest. Roofs are virtually free of any nonavian predators, and they don't get overwashed by storm-driven waves. You won't find that kind of security with a nest on the beach.

Whatever the reason, the birds certainly have taken to the roofs. For example, our surveys show that about 75 percent of the least tern colonies and nests in Florida now occur on roofs. Black skimmers are less common roof-nesters, and they are typically less successful in producing young on roofs. Since they are larger birds, they often scrape nests so deep into the gravel that they crack their eggs on the hard substrate.

Most coastal cities in Florida, and even some inland, have a number of buildings with roof-nesting birds. Occupied roofs can be near the ocean or several miles from the water, and buildings of all sizes are used. Although most birds nest on one- or two-story buildings, some choose roofs that are seven or more stories high.

Getting on a roof to watch nesting birds is not practical and disrupts the birds, but if you're observant you should be able to see least terns flying to and from a roof. Look or listen in spring and summer for terns or skimmers flying noisily above any flat-roofed buildings. Or check for the distinctive whitewash they leave on the pavement and awnings. If you're lucky, you may be able to watch them feed and drink from a nearby canal, lake, or water retention pond. Wherever you see them, enjoy the sight of these adaptable birds that have learned to use any suitable beach habitat, even one on top of a Wal-Mart!

Bittern and Bobwhite Cluster

56. Lake Proctor Wilderness Area 85

57. Geneva Wilderness Area 85

58. Little Big Econ State Forest: Kilbee Tract 86

59. Little Big Econ State Forest: Demetree Tract 86

60. Orlando Wetlands Park 87

61. Tosohatchee State Reserve 88

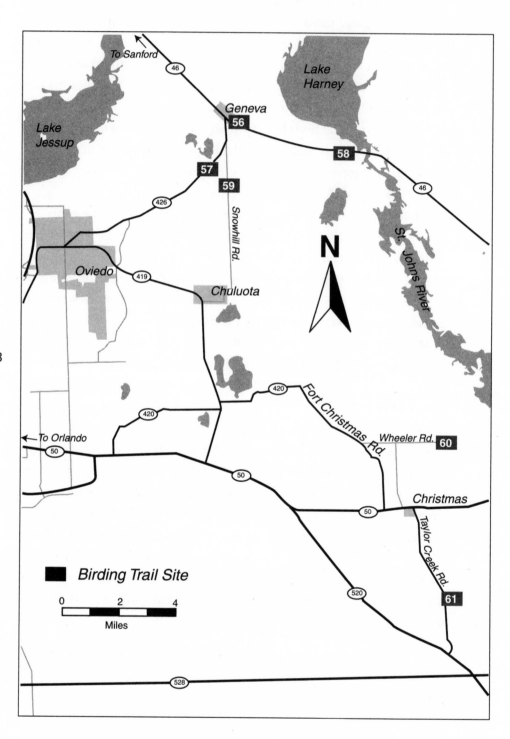

56. Lake Proctor Wilderness Area

DESCRIPTION: An acquisition of the Seminole County Natural Lands Program, the Lake Proctor Wilderness Area offers an opportunity to hike and bird more than six miles of trails through flatwoods, sandhill, and oak hammock habitats, as well as a vantage of Lake Proctor. Pick up a brochure at the entrance for a site map and description of which habitats occur in which parts of the property. As you might expect, the hammocks and flatwoods are good for groups of migrants in fall and spring; wading birds, including nesting sandhill cranes, frequent the lake. Watch the lake margin for skulking waterbirds, like snipe and bittern, hiding in the vegetation. Raptors and sparrows favor the open grassy area on the power-line easement. Educational programs are available weekdays to groups of ten to thirty people. Call for details and reservations.

DIRECTIONS: From Sanford, take SR 46 east. Go one mile past the intersection with CR 426 and the site will be on the left (north) side of the road.

Open sunrise to sunset. Best months for birding are September–April.

(407) 665-7352.

www.co.seminole.fl.us/natland/proctor.htm.

57. Geneva Wilderness Area

DESCRIPTION: Another part of Seminole County's innovative natural lands program, the Geneva Wilderness Area offers a pleasant hiking and birding experience through scrubby flatwoods peppered with seasonal ponds. Listen and watch for eastern towhees scratching in the leaf litter and for mixed flocks of kinglets and warblers in the oaks in fall, winter, and spring. The ponds have sandhill cranes and the whole suite of Florida wading birds, plus snipe and ducks including wood ducks and hooded mergansers. Pick up a map at the entrance kiosk and bring water. Educational programs are available for groups; call for details, availability, and reservations.

DIRECTIONS: From Oviedo, take CR 426 northeast six miles. The site is on the right (southeast) side of the road. If you reach Snowhill Road, you have gone too far.

Open sunrise to sunset. Best months for birding are September–April.

(407) 665-7352

www.co.seminole.fl.us/natland/geneva.htm.

58 and 59. Little Big Econ State Forest

DESCRIPTION: This property has two tracts that are good for birding. The Demetree Tract off Snowhill Road has a parking area surrounded by improved pasture, and a visitor center with maps and forest information. Start by birding the pasture for meadowlarks, bluebirds, sparrows, and raptors, then follow the trail southwest to the river boardwalk. A trail snakes along and through the treeline that follows the Econlockhatchee River, offering excellent birding for a diversity of resident and migratory songbirds like summer tanagers, blue grosbeaks, black-throated blue warblers, and Philadelphia vireos. Pick up a map at the entrance station and take water for your hike. The other promising birding spot is the Kilbee Tract, which abuts the St. Johns River. Drive partway into the property and then hike the entrance road the one mile to the end where the floodplain opens, offering a view of the river and its waders, shorebirds, and ducks in fall and winter. The walk itself is unremarkable, so you might scope the river from the boat launch at the SR 46 bridge. If it looks like birding the river would be productive, then the hike is definitely worthwhile. The trail is in full sun, so plan accordingly. There is some hunting on the property from October through December.

DIRECTIONS: From Oviedo, take CR 426 to Snowhill Road. Turn right (south) and go one mile to reach the Demetree Tract entrance (site 59) on the right (west) side of the road. For the Kilbee Tract (site 58), take CR 426 to SR 46. Turn right (east) and go 4.3 miles. Entrance to the Kilbee Tract is on the right (south) side of SR 46 just before the St. Johns River bridge.

Open 8:00 A.M. to sunset. Best months for birding are September–April.

(407) 971-3500.

www.fl-dof.com.

60. Orlando Wetlands Park

DESCRIPTION: Orlando Wetlands Park is a large treatment facility that uses water plants to polish already treated wastewater before discharging it into the St. Johns River. This prevents algae blooms in the St. Johns and provides a fertile habitat for all kinds of wetlands wildlife. Wading birds like snowy egrets and glossy ibis are common here, as are both bitterns and purple gallinules. Osprey feed throughout the wetland complex, and purple martins nest in tree cavities each spring—one of the only places east of the Mississippi where they nest in anything other than man-made houses! A trail that begins at the parking lot and winds east around Lake Searcy and north through a hammock can be good for migratory songbirds in season. Watch for ducks and shorebirds in the wetlands in fall and winter, and large flocks of migratory tree swallows coming in to roost in late fall and early spring. Hiking is, for the most part, on raised, exposed dikes. Plan for full sun and insects, and watch for summer thunderstorms. Large alligators also inhabit these wetlands, and may bask on the dikes. While no cause for alarm, they should be neither approached nor fed. THIS PROPERTY IS CLOSED SEASONALLY, FROM OCTOBER 1 UNTIL JANUARY 20 EACH YEAR.

DIRECTIONS: From Orlando, take SR 50 east to the town of Christmas. Turn left (north) onto Fort Christmas Road (CR 420) and go 2.3 miles to Wheeler Road, a dirt road leading off to the right (east). Take this for 1.5 miles. The parking area will be on your left. Please pick up a map and sign in.

Open sunrise to sunset. Best months for birding are September–April.

(407) 568-1706.

61. Tosohatchee State Reserve

DESCRIPTION: A large, wild tract of land that abuts the St. Johns River, Tosohatchee State Reserve offers a diversity of habitats from hydric hammock to wetlands to gorgeous flatwoods. Stop at the entrance kiosk and pick up a bird list and map. Also check for road closures. The majority of this property's dirt roads can be driven in a two-wheel-drive vehicle; if roads are wet or too sandy, the roads are closed to vehicular traffic. Drive Powerline Road slowly looking for raptors, bluebirds, turkeys, and sparrows. While crossing the Jim Creek slough, watch for waders like wood storks and limpkins. The road ends at the St. Johns River in a marsh where rails, ducks, and purple gallinules can be found. Occasionally a crested caracara can be seen at the end of the road. Flatwoods on the north and south ends of the property are good for brown-headed nuthatches and warblers. The approximately sixty miles of rustic trails in the interior offer a good opportunity for migratory songbirds; be sure to take a map and water, and be prepared for insects. There is some hunting on this property, so call ahead or check at the kiosk.

DIRECTIONS: From Orlando, take SR 50 east to the town of Christmas. Turn right (south) on Taylor Creek Road. Proceed three miles and the reserve entrance will be on the left (east) side of the road.

Open 8:00 A.M. to sunset. Best months for birding are October–April.

(407) 568-5893.

www.dep.state.fl.us/parks.

Gateway to the Great Florida Birding Trail

Merritt Island National Wildlife Refuge

Joanna Taylor

Mention Kennedy Space Center and many people imagine the excitement of a countdown and the thrill of the liftoff. However, there is another kind of "space" on Merritt Island, one that is almost unknown to outsiders.

The United States Fish and Wildlife Service has the unique distinction of managing the habitats of the National Aeronautical and Space Administration's John F. Kennedy Space Center. In fact, only 5 percent of the land is designated for NASA's space operations; the other 95 percent is managed for wildlife under the auspices of Merritt Island National Wildlife Refuge and Canaveral National Seashore. One might ask, how could the world's leading center of space technology coexist peacefully with nature? Actually, it is because of NASA that this barrier island remains undeveloped and so valuable for Florida's wildlife.

Merritt Island National Wildlife Refuge, the second largest refuge in Florida, is located on a unique barrier island consisting of 140,000 acres of salt marshes, freshwater impoundments, brackish estuaries, hardwood hammocks, pine flatwoods, Florida scrub, and pristine beaches. Blessed with these diverse habitats, Merritt Island remains unsurpassed as a refuge for endangered species: it supports twenty-one wildlife species listed as endangered or threatened, more than any other single refuge in the United States.

Located where the subtropical and temperate climatic zones meet, Merritt Island and its surrounding waterways encompass ecosystems teeming with life, including the Indian River Lagoon, named as one of North America's most biologically productive estuaries. Strategically located on the Eastern Continental Flyway, a major bird migration corridor, the refuge is a key resting and feeding stop for many migrating bird species.

The cool, sunny days of November usher in the peak season for bird-watching at the refuge. As birds migrate south along the coast, they stop when they reach the fertile wetlands of the refuge and the protection offered by the undeveloped barrier island. Merritt Island is considered one of the state's prime birding sites: more than 330 species of birds can be found on the wildlife refuge, including the Florida scrub-jay, roseate spoonbill, reddish egret, American wood stork, white pelican, bald eagle, American avocet, black-necked stilt, and northern pintail.

Birding a variety of habitats on the refuge can be exceptionally rewarding, particularly from November through March. Impoundments and salt marshes offer the most diversified viewing opportunities, including wading birds, shorebirds, waterfowl, gulls, terns, rails, sparrows, blackbirds, and raptors. In the refuge's hardwood hammocks, you'll find excellent birding for warblers and other songbirds during the fall and spring migration. The pine flatwoods host breeding populations of bald eagles, which nest annually in the large pine trees in the winter months. One of the last three stronghold populations of the threatened Florida scrub-jay are found in the refuge's fire-dependent scrub habitat. Finally, forty-three miles of pristine dune and beach habitat draw in sanderlings, willets, red knots, ruddy turnstones, black-bellied plovers, gulls and terns, and other shorebirds.

Together, the refuge, seashore, and NASA form a sheltered space, where the countdown is not only for spaceships but also for many endangered plants and animals that need this landscape to ensure their continued existence. The unique relationship the refuge shares with NASA bears testimony to the idea that nature and technology can peacefully coexist.

Third Subsection Map

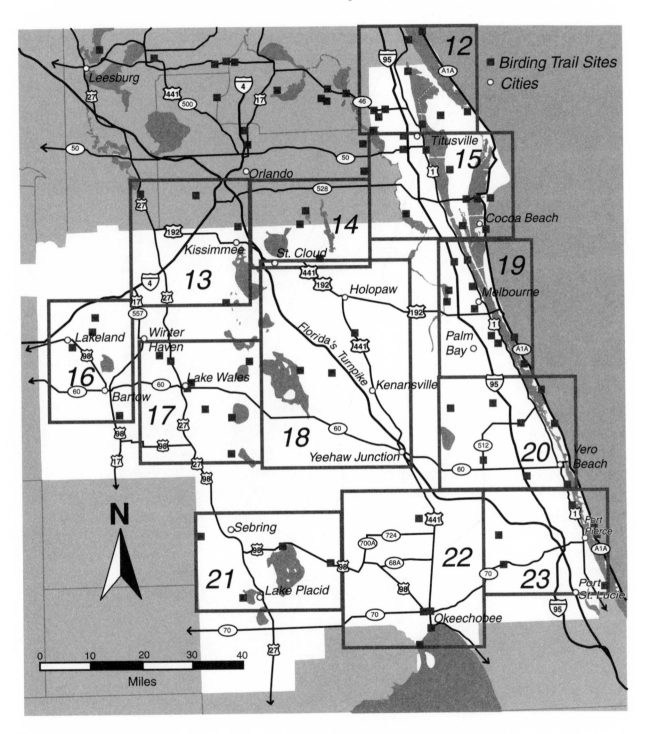

Birding Trail Sites
Cities

Leesburg
Orlando
Titusville
Cocoa Beach
Kissimmee
St. Cloud
Holopaw
Melbourne
Lakeland
Winter Haven
Lake Wales
Kenansville
Palm Bay
Bartow
Yeehaw Junction
Vero Beach
Sebring
Lake Placid
Okeechobee
Port Pierce
Port St. Lucie

Florida's Turnpike

N

Miles

12 15 14 19 13 16 17 18 20 21 22 23

River to Ocean Cluster

62. Merritt Island National Wildlife Refuge 93

63. Canaveral National Seashore (North Entrance) 93

64. River Breeze Park 94

65. Scottsmoor Landing 95

66. Buck Lake Conservation Area (West Entrance) 95

67. Buck Lake Conservation Area (East Entrance) 95

68. Seminole Ranch Conservation Area 96

69. Parrish Park–Titusville 97

70. Canaveral National Seashore (South Entrance) 97

71. Hatbill Park 98

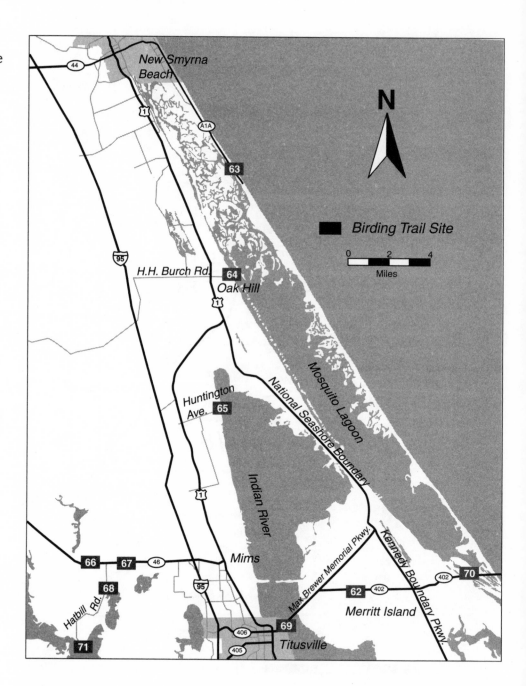

62. Merritt Island National Wildlife Refuge

DESCRIPTION: Merritt Island National Wildlife Refuge is a premier birding site—world-renowned for its Black Point Wildlife Drive, its shorebird and wading bird opportunities can't be beat. Fall and winter are best for these species, but even in summer, Florida specialties such as roseate spoonbills and scrub-jays aren't hard to find. Drive Black Point slowly, scanning for rails and a diversity of ducks like pintails, shovelers, and teal, and sorting through the flocks of shorebirds loafing on the flats. Reddish egrets occasionally "dance" in the shallows as they hunt for prey, and northern harriers will flush the shorebirds in winter, mixing the group so you can see that one frustrating bird that was hiding at the back. The hammock and scrub trails are popular and during migrations have been known to turn up surprises, like a Townsend's warbler in spring 2000. Florida scrub-jays are best seen on telephone wires and posts on Kennedy Boundary Parkway in the refuge. Guided birding trips appropriate for beginners and experts alike occur weekly, November through March. Check in at the visitor center for information on all of the refuge's opportunities, and check the log for recent bird sightings in the area.

DIRECTIONS: Take I-95 to SR 406 at Titusville. Go east on SR 406 across the Indian River. Stay right as SR 406 veers left. The Visitor Center will be approximately four miles on the right.

Visitor Center open Monday through Friday, 8:00 A.M. to 4:30 P.M.; Saturday and Sunday, 9:00 A.M. to 5:00 P.M.; closed Sundays, April through October. Refuge open sunrise to sunset. Closed during NASA shuttle launches. Best months for birding are October–May.

(321) 861-0667.

www.nbbd.com/godo/minwr.

63. Canaveral National Seashore (North Entrance)

DESCRIPTION: At Canaveral National Seashore the barrier island preserve offers a rich array of birding pleasures: access to the beach for shorebirds, terns, and gulls; elevated platforms on the dune line to scope for migrating raptors along the shore, and gannets and jaegers out at sea; winding trails through maritime hammock for painted buntings and migratory songbirds; and vantages of the lagoon where waders, shorebirds, and rafts of migratory ducks seek shelter and feed. Get a map at the entrance station and a bird checklist at the information center. This center's parking lot is an easy access to the lagoon as your first stop. At the last parking area, a dike trail leads off to the south for twelve miles, allowing a wilder birding experience, viewing the lagoon, beach, and coastal scrub. This property is one of the best sites in Florida to scope offshore for seabirds such as jaegers. Guided tours and programs are available, so call ahead for details or check the information center for a schedule when you arrive.

DIRECTIONS: From I-95 in New Smyrna, take SR 44 east to SR A1A. Turn right (south) and drive seven miles on A1A to the park entrance.

Open 6:00 A.M. to 8:00 P.M. in summer, 6:00 A.M. to 6:00 P.M. in winter. Best months for birding are September–April.

(386) 867-4077.

www.nbbd.com/godo/cns.

64. River Breeze Park

DESCRIPTION: The unique feature of the small county park called River Breeze is a keyhole dock that extends out into Mosquito Lagoon. At high tide the area may seem unremarkable, but at low tide its mudflats are exposed in and around the keyhole, where shorebirds like avocets, dunlin, red knots, and dowitchers feed close to the viewers above. This is a good site to practice shorebird identification in fall and winter at low tide, when exposed bars also host loafing terns, gulls, pelicans, and waders like roseate spoonbills. Check your tide tables the night before your visit so you can plan your route accordingly.

DIRECTIONS: From US 1 in Oak Hill, turn east on H. H. Burch Road. The site is located at the end of the road on the left (north) side.

Open sunrise to sunset. Best months for birding are September–April.

(386) 345-5525.

65. Scottsmoor Landing

Description: If you're in the area, Scottsmoor Landing is worth a look. At this access to northern Indian River Lagoon, you can scope in winter for migratory ducks, loons, and horned grebes. Shorebirds and waders line the shore, and northern harriers prowl the black needle rush marsh, where rails skulk in the tall reeds. Watch for painted buntings on the dirt road into the park.

Directions: From Mims, take US 1 north of SR 46 for eight miles. Go east a mile and a half on Huntington Avenue. The park is at the end of the road on the river.

Open sunrise to sunset. Best months for birding are October–May.

(321) 264-5105.

www.brevardparks.com.

66 and 67. Buck Lake Conservation Area

Description: The wild Buck Lake Conservation Area is fruitful if you invest time and energy in hiking its extensive uplands. Sought-after species occurring here include Bachman's sparrows (in the easternmost quarter of the property), brown-headed nuthatches, Florida scrub-jays, turkeys, eastern bluebirds, red-headed woodpeckers, and migrants like blue grosbeaks. Migratory months are most productive and most comfortable. Be aware that there is also some hunting on the property during these times, so call for hunt dates or check the entrance kiosks before you bird. This property is large and wild, so be sure to pick up a map at the kiosk, and take water along on your hike.

DIRECTIONS: From Mims, take SR 46 west past I-95 and proceed approximately two miles to entrance on the right (north) side of the road. A second entrance to the property is another five miles west on the north side of the road.

Open sunrise to sunset. Best months for birding are October–April.

For hunt information, call (904) 329-4404.

http://sjr.state.fl.us.

68. Seminole Ranch Conservation Area

DESCRIPTION: The 28,000-acre Seminole Ranch Conservation Area, like Buck Lake, yields the best experience when time and energy are invested in hiking the property's extensive trail system. Its hammocks and wetlands are thick with everything from migratory songbirds and painted buntings to turkeys and wading birds. King, clapper, and sora rails, among others, can be found in the marshes where the property borders the St. Johns River. There is traditionally hunting on the south portion in fall and winter, but the directions here are to the northern, no-hunt portions of the property. Hike the hammocks in the early morning; the ability to identify birdcalls can be particularly helpful at this site. There are several entrances on the west side of the road, with map kiosks at each. As they will mention, be sure to take water and insect repellent, especially in warmer months.

DIRECTIONS: From Mims, take SR 46 approximately eight miles west from I-95. Turn south on Hatbill Road. There are several trailheads on the west side of the road as you drive down Hatbill Road. Map kiosks are posted at each trailhead.

Open sunrise to sunset. Best months for birding are February–April, October–December.

http://sjr.state.fl.us.

69. Parrish Park–Titusville

DESCRIPTION: Adjacent to Merritt Island National Wildlife Refuge, Parrish Park–Titusville offers an excellent vantage of Indian River Lagoon. It is a highly seasonal site, providing spectacular views of a variety of wintering ducks, shorebirds, loons, and horned grebes in fall and winter. Check both sides of the road for loafing terns and black skimmers, ruddy turnstones and other shorebirds. This is one of the most reliable sites in winter for greater black-backed gulls. Dabbling ducks like to form "rafts" as they cluster together in Indian River Lagoon, and may congregate in the wind shadow of islands and in coves. Diving ducks, loons, and grebes are more likely to be feeding in loose groups in the lagoon; a spotting scope can be helpful in viewing all of these birds. In spring and summer, little will be seen at this site except gulls, terns, and some wading birds, so stop by for a peek, but then move on to more fruitful warm-weather birding at Merritt Island.

DIRECTIONS: From Titusville, take SR 406 across the Indian River. After crossing, the park is immediately on your left (north).

Open sunrise to sunset. Best months for birding are October–May.

(321) 264-5105.

www.brevardparks.com.

70. Canaveral National Seashore (South Entrance)

DESCRIPTION: Adjacent to Merritt Island National Wildlife Refuge, the National Seashore fills out your birding day list with beach species such as plovers, turnstones, terns, and gulls. And watch immediately after the entrance station for Florida scrub-jays on either side of the road. Osprey, anhingas, and eagles are also common on the drive in. Park at a beach crossover and bird the beach, watching offshore for the occasional pelagic bird such as gannet or jaeger. Sea ducks, loons, and cormorants feed in the surf in winter. Call the seashore's headquarters for scheduled educational programming during your visit.

Directions: From Titusville, take SR 406 east and veer right (east) onto SR 402. Proceed through Merritt Island National Wildlife Refuge to the Canaveral National Seashore entrance station.

Open 6:00 A.M. to 8:00 P.M. in summer, 6:00 A.M. to 6:00 P.M. in winter. Best months for birding are January–December.

(321) 867-4077.

www.nbbd.com/godo/cns.

71. Hatbill Park

Description: The drive to Hatbill Park passes through parts of Seminole Ranch Conservation Area, so watch the roadside for everything from songbird migrants to turkeys. Hatbill Park itself is on the St. Johns River, providing an excellent view of hundreds of wading birds coming in to roost at sunset. White and glossy ibis, snowy egrets, great egrets, and tricolored herons all pass by in squadrons, bound for roost sites in the estuary. In winter, rafts of ducks and flocks of swallows are visible near sunset, and by bringing your own kayak, you can access the river from this point. Prowl for owls along the road on the way back. This site can get busy on weekends, when it is used as a boat launch and fishing spot. Also, be prepared for biting insects.

Directions: From Mims, take SR 46 west from I-95 for 4.2 miles to Hatbill Road, a dirt road on the left (south) side of SR 46. Take Hatbill Road several miles to the park at the end.

Open sunrise to sunset. Best months for birding are October–April.

(321) 264-5105.

www.brevardparks.com.

Demise of the Dusky

Jim Cox

Sparrows in an open field tax many a birder's skill, but marsh dwellers like the dusky seaside sparrow are more challenging still. To people passing through the marshy habitat of the dusky prior to its extinction in 1987, the bird was probably a small dark blur at best. My first look at a dusky required lots of patience. I was trying to look at the bird through two chain-linked fences, the innermost covered with thick cane matting. The mat served as a blind, shielding one of only two males of this subspecies known to be alive at the time. The bird played coy, anticipating my moves, going in the opposite direction, until I was granted a quick half-second glimpse as it fluttered past a break in the matting. The irony of this caged bird being the first seaside sparrow I'd ever seen was not lost upon me.

The dusky seaside sparrow dwelled only in Florida's Brevard County along the floodplain of the St. Johns River, and in the salt marshes surrounding Merritt Island. The bird's choice of habitat in freshwater marshes was unusual: except for the endangered Cape Sable seaside sparrow living in freshwater marshes of the Florida Everglades, all other seaside sparrows use salt marshes exclusively.

Homesteading in freshwater marshes certainly helped to prolong life for the dusky because salt marshes on Merritt Island were hardest hit initially as the Kennedy Space Center and other developments began in the area. Spraying of the pesticide DDT to control mosquitoes began in the 1940s and quickly reduced sparrow populations by an estimated 70 percent. As mosquitoes developed a resistance to DDT, an even more deadly form of insect control was devised: the impoundment and diking of all the coastal marshes of Brevard County. By 1968, in response to the destruction of their habitat, all but thirty dusky seaside sparrows had been extirpated from Merritt Island.

At this same time, about eight hundred pairs still occurred in marshes along the St. Johns River. Before the end of the decade, habitat alterations quickly eliminated this population as well. Two new roads were constructed through the heart of the sparrows' range, draining much of the marsh they used. Canals also were dug for development in another area, and even though land was purchased as a refuge in hopes of saving the birds, the canals were not filled quickly enough. Then a series of wildfires jumped onto the refuge from neighboring private lands, and by 1980 the population was reduced to only four individuals. At that time, these last few birds were removed from the wild to a captive breeding program in Orlando.

The dusky seaside sparrow was described as a distinct species when it was first discovered in 1872. It was merged with the other North American seaside sparrows in 1973, despite the fact that the dusky looked distinctive and was isolated from the other sparrows with which it shared its scientific name. This "lumping" was based on other good biological criteria, but according to Dr. Herb Kale, chief ornithologist at the Florida Audubon Society until his death in 1995, the merger had disastrous ramifications. In 1995 Kale said that "suddenly, a vast growing constituency of bird watchers with an interest and urgency to see and save the bird vanished."

The extinction of the dusky in the summer of 1987 is a dark blemish on human stewardship of wildlife in Florida. Dredged marshes were not restored, roads were laid in the wrong places, fires burned too long, and a captive breeding program was started much too late. We can only hope that the dusky's demise has enlightened us and will prompt better caretaking of rare species in the future.

Natural Attractions Cluster

72. Lake Louisa State Park   102

73. Tibet-Butler Preserve   102

74. Gatorland   103

75. The Nature Conservancy's Disney Wilderness Preserve   104

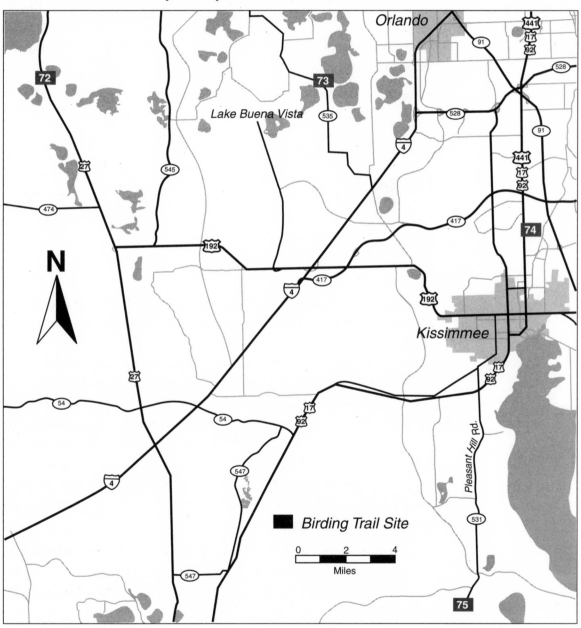

72. Lake Louisa State Park

DESCRIPTION: Lake Louisa is worth a stop if you're traveling US 27 between Clermont and Haines City. Traditionally, the only access to the state park was from the west, and it offered marginal birding opportunities. Recently a new entrance has been added off US 27, making it possible to stop in briefly, bird the lake at the end of the road, and watch for grassland species like sparrows, meadowlarks, turkeys, bobwhite, and raptors on the way in and out. There are more extensive, rustic trails available for those interested in exploring.

DIRECTIONS: From I-4, travel fifteen miles north on US 27. The entrance will be on the left (west) side of the road.

Open 8:00 A.M. to sunset. Best months for birding are September–April.

(352) 394-3969.

www.dep.state.fl.us/parks.

73. Tibet-Butler Preserve

DESCRIPTION: A county park that fronts on Lake Tibet-Butler and shelters great pine flatwoods, a bayhead swamp, and oak hammocks—what more could a birder ask for? Its gorgeous nature center provides a quick orientation to the area to help you decide which route to follow. Hike to the waterfront for wading bird species like white ibis and anhinga? Or walk the bayhead, hammocks, and flatwoods for songbird migrants? Their bird list has a respectable eleven warblers, and that's just a start. Watch overhead for swallow-tailed kites in spring and summer. This preserve provides an incredible diversity of educational programs, including a Breakfast with the Birds program. Be sure to call in advance for a schedule, or to make reservations for your group. A stone's throw from Lake Buena Vista, Tibet-Butler Preserve shows what was here before the theme parks.

DIRECTIONS: From I-4 on the south side of Orlando, take the exit for Lake Buena Vista and go west on SR 535. Drive through the first light. At the second, turn left; SR 535 turns with you. Follow this road north approximately five and one-half miles. Tibet-Butler Preserve will be on the right (north) side of the road.

Open Wednesday through Sunday, 8:00 A.M. to 6:00 P.M. Best months for birding are October–April.

(407)876-6696.

http://parks.orangecountyfl.net.

74. Gatorland

DESCRIPTION: Gatorland was one of Florida's first tourist attractions, and wading birds flock to this site for the same reason people do: the alligators. Wading birds in the wild choose to nest over water, so that alligators can live beneath their nests, protecting them from marauders like raccoons. Accordingly, wild wading birds—great blue, little blue, green, and tricolored herons, black-crowned night herons, white ibis, wood storks, snowy egrets—have been nesting over the alligator ponds at Gatorland for years. Boardwalks wind through this area, and the birds are very habituated to people. Viewers can stand just a few feet from birds and their young without disturbing them. Great for photography, working out your wading bird identification, or just marveling at the ugly beauty of baby birds. The birds nest from January to August, with the peak between April and June. Tell the admission counter you're with the Great Florida Birding Trail.

DIRECTIONS: Located three miles north of Kissimmee on South Orange Blossom Trail (US 441), Gatorland is on the east side of the road.

Open 9:00 A.M. to 6:00 P.M. in winter, 9:00 A.M. to 7:00 P.M. in summer. Best months for birding are January, August–December.

(407) 855-5496.

www.gatorland.com.

75. The Nature Conservancy's Disney Wilderness Preserve

DESCRIPTION: The Disney Wilderness Preserve represents a unique partnership between the Walt Disney Corporation and the Nature Conservancy. Required to pay mitigation credits for developments near Lake Buena Vista, Disney's dollars went into the purchase and management of this beautiful 12,000–acre tract of land. The Nature Conservancy has constructed an excellent educational facility on-site, along with seven miles of trails for hiking. Watch for turkeys and sandhill cranes on the drive in. Florida sandhill cranes, a subspecies, typically feed in pairs or small family groups. Larger groups of sandhills which you may see in winter represent migratory cranes overwintering in Florida. On the trail, expect raptors, bobwhite, wrens, warblers, bluebirds, and sparrows. At the lake margins, woodcocks, waders, snipe, king rails, and ducks have been seen. Florida scrub-jays are resident on the south end of the property as well, accessible by special tours only. Tours and programs are available for groups with advance reservations; call for details.

DIRECTIONS: From Kissimmee, take John Young Parkway south to Pleasant Hill Road. After eight miles, as you enter Poinciana, turn left onto Old Pleasant Hill Road. The preserve entrance is the left (east) side of the road.

Open 9:00 A.M. to 5:00 P.M. Opens at 7:00 A.M. on Saturdays, January–March. Best months for birding are January–April, October–November.

(407) 935-0002.

www.tncflorida.org.

www.nature.org/florida.

Burning for Birds

Why Birders Should Support the Use of Prescribed Fire

R. Todd Engstrom

All naturalists and wildlife enthusiasts should be on the lookout for an increasingly rare bird: the phoenix. This ancient mythical creature is periodically consumed in flames and rises reborn from the ashes, symbolizing a critical fact for Florida wildlife: many of our most distinctive bird species live in plant communities that depend on fire.

The list of Florida's "birds of fire" reads like a who's who of rare and endangered species of the state. The Florida scrub-jay, the only bird species solely endemic to Florida, fares best in scrub habitat that is burned every eight to twenty years. The federally listed endangered red-cockaded woodpecker—27 percent of its entire population occurs in Florida—and its habitat associates, the Bachman's sparrow and the brown-headed nuthatch, depend on open mature pinelands, which are burned at even shorter intervals. Long-term maintenance of high-quality habitat for these species more than offsets the loss of a few nests in any single year caused by the application of prescribed fire. The Florida grasshopper sparrow, a subspecies residing in central Florida, and wintering populations of the rapidly declining Henslow's sparrow, use savannahs that are shaped by fire. And, although it seems counterintuitive, freshwater marshes that provide habitat for the Florida sandhill crane, the recently reintroduced whooping crane, the wood stork, and the Cape Sable seaside sparrow are strongly influenced by fire.

Few direct measures exist of how often Florida's ecosystems burned before humans arrived in the Southeast, and we have poor knowledge of Native American use of fire. Clues, such as the signature left by pollen of ancient plant communities in layers of mud, and accounts of early Spanish and French explorers, provide rudimentary understanding, but nothing definitive. When fire is removed from natural ecosystems of Florida, however, we learn a vivid lesson in the dynamics of plant succession. Suppression of fire from forest ecosystems that frequently experience fire will typically result in transition from a forest or savannah characterized by an open canopy, composed of pines and a rich variety of herbs and grasses, to a closed-canopy forest dominated by shrubs and hardwoods with relatively little ground cover. In freshwater marshes, fire slows the buildup of organic soil and the advance of shrubs and trees. These are profound alterations to the structure and composition of bird habitat.

The response of the avian community to fire exclusion is as dramatic as are changes to the vegetation. If fires are not permitted to burn in naturally open habitats, birds such as the eastern kingbird, loggerhead shrike, and eastern meadowlark will rapidly disappear. Blue grosbeak and indigo bunting, species that prefer open habitats with scattered bushes, would vanish next. Wetland birds, such as bitterns, common yellowthroats, and red-winged blackbirds that rely on grassy vegetation for nesting habitat, and thousands of wading birds that forage in marshes would be affected by fire suppression. It is true that other bird species would move into vegetation altered by the elimination of fire, but at the same time Florida would likely lose some of its most valued residents.

Lightning-ignited fire was a major force that shaped the ecosystems of Florida long before any humans arrived, and it was undoubtedly used by Native Americans for agriculture and to manage wildlife. Today, we introduce fire into a landscape fragmented by roads, cities, and highly modified environments. Fire is prescribed by land managers to maintain certain habitats, after careful consideration of weather and fuel conditions. Prescribed fire is an agent of renewal that is essential to the long-term perpetuation of many of Florida's most distinctive ecosystems, and the birds and other wildlife that live there.

Turkey Cluster

76. Moss Park   108

77. Split Oak Mitigation Park   108

78. Lake Lizzie Nature Preserve   109

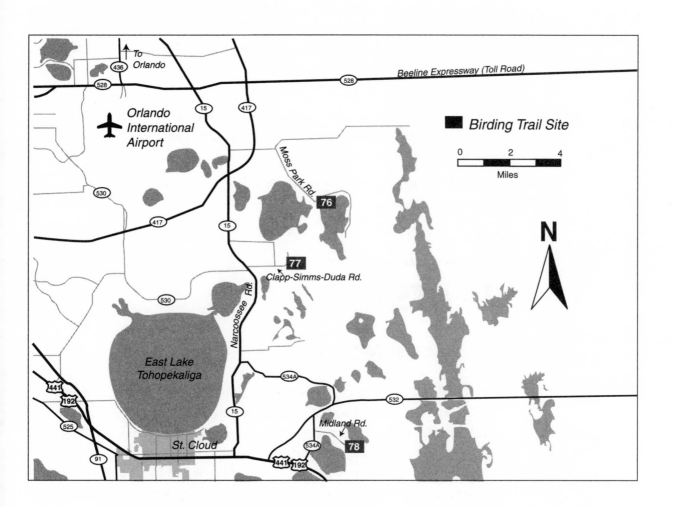

76. Moss Park

DESCRIPTION: Orange County's large Moss Park offers a diversity of birding experiences: wander the oak hammock for sandhill cranes and wild turkeys; scope the island in the middle of Lake Mary Jane in summer to watch the wood storks nesting there; check the large field at the south end of the property for raptors; hike the wooded edges looking for migratory songbirds in season. If you choose to stay the night and camp, prowl for owls and listen for whippoorwills, chuck-will's-widows, and nighthawks. Adjacent to the wilder Split Oak Mitigation Park, you could camp here in comfort and explore Split Oak's wilderness at your leisure. Programs and guided hikes are available for groups if you call in advance. The park also hosts the Wading Bird Festival early every May.

DIRECTIONS: From SR 436 just north of the Orlando International Airport, take Hoffner Road (which becomes Narcoossee Road/SR 15) east, then southeast, for eight miles to Moss Park Road. Turn left (east) onto Moss Park Road and follow it four miles to the park at the end.

Open 8:00 A.M. to 6:00 P.M. in winter, 8:00 A.M. to 7:30 P.M. in summer. Best months for birding are January–December.

(407) 273-2327.

http://parks.orangecountyfl.net.

77. Split Oak Mitigation Park

DESCRIPTION: A wild tract acquired as mitigation for development elsewhere in Central Florida, Split Oak Mitigation Park was purchased primarily to protect the upland habitats crucial to the survival of the gopher tortoise. Birding this property takes some time and some hiking. Head south from the entrance, across the improved pasture and into the oak hammock, looking for turkeys and songbirds. The southeast corner of the property is particularly good for migrants in season. If you walk due east into the scrubby oaks from the parking area, several warbler windows open up in the trees and can be good in migration. The north and northeastern edges of the property are bordered by wetlands where wading birds flourish. Be sure to pick up a map before hiking, and bring whatever water you will need for a long, warm hike. Split Oak is also accessible from the east side, via Moss Park, at times of low water. Ask at Moss Park for directions. This access is the most convenient if your goal is to see Split Oak's namesake tree, which grows in the northeast corner of the property.

DIRECTIONS: From Orlando, take Narcoossee Road (CR 15) or the Beeline Expressway (SR 528) east. From the intersection of SR 528 and CR 15, go seven miles south on CR 15. Turn left (east) on Clapp-Simms-Duda Road and follow signs to the entrance.

Open dawn to dusk. Best months for birding are October–April.

(863)648-3203.

78. Lake Lizzie Nature Preserve

DESCRIPTION: An Osceola County preserve, Lake Lizzie has a large number of trails, so pick up a map at the entrance to the property or at the County Zoning Department in Kissimmee. Follow the main trail to the south, make the first turn to the east, and curve back north again to follow the power line past Trout Lake and its wetlands. Watch for raptors, wrens, sparrows, and wading birds on this route. Due south from the parking area, some patches of wet prairie with bayheads shelter nesting sandhill cranes and wetland species like snipe and woodcock. The entire preserve is good for migratory songbirds; in a good morning's hike you can see a diversity of species including ruby-crowned kinglets, northern parulas, pine, prairie, and palm warblers, summer tanagers, American goldfinches, and all of Florida's woodpeckers except for the red-cockaded. Take water and a map with you when you hike this property. Summer can be uncomfortably hot, and biting insects can be pesky.

DIRECTIONS: From St. Cloud, take US 192 east to Bass Highway (CR 534A). Turn left (north) and go to Midland Road. Turn right and follow the road to the park at the end.

Open sunrise to sunset. Best months for birding are October–April.

(407)343-3400 or (407) 343-3409.

Birdwatching 101

Birding by Ear

Jim Cox

Mozart liked to hang out with good musicians. One of his scores includes a revision proposed by none other than his pet bird, a starling. The bird imitated a passage quite closely, but flattened a couple of notes, to which Wolfgang wrote, "That was beautiful."

The music of people clearly has its counterpart in the music of birds, but our enjoyment is incidental to the main purpose of birdsongs. Birds are musical marvels simply to express the important things they have to say, from "Get out of here!" to "You look great!"

When most people think of bird music, they are thinking of birdsongs as opposed to birdcalls. The difference may seem technical, but an understanding helps to appreciate the full range of musical offerings found in the avian world. Calls are short, innate vocalizations that serve as warning calls or help to maintain contact while migrating. Raise a bird in isolation, and its calls will be similar to other members of the species. Songs, on the other hand, are learned and much more complex. If you raise a bird in isolation, it will not develop a proper song. The vocalizations will be a disorganized jumble barely recognizable as the song of that species. Songs are not found throughout the avian world but are limited to about 45 percent of all birds.

Most songbirds learn their tunes in the time-honored way of folk musicians, namely by ear. A young songbird sitting in a nest or a bush hears its parent singing, and it matches that tune to a mental model of the tune that sits in its head. The mental model helps the bird filter out songs of other birds that might also influence it. The young bird then practices the song as it grows, listening to its parents singing, and trying to match the phrasing and timbre, but also possibly incorporating variants used by neighbors. So, much like the practiced flautist, the male cardinal bursting forth in song is showing off months of hard work as well as innate talent.

Songs usually serve at least two important functions: to defend a territory, and to attract a mate. Songs stimulate egg production in many female birds and provide a perfect means of communicating over long distances. Birds also have individual phrases and cadences that enable their neighbors to recognize that "Fred" is singing in that tree over there, while "Charlie" is going on a bit off-key in the bushes. If some stranger bumbles into a well-delineated neighborhood of territories and starts in without an invitation, it is likely to be mobbed by everyone.

Local dialects also occur, as you would expect in any practice with a strong learning component. Red-winged blackbirds in south Florida sound different from those in north Florida, and some species even change the pitch of their songs with their surroundings. A high-pitched version of the song carries better in a dense forest, while a lower-pitched version might work best in an open field.

Many birds also learn new song variants as they age, and some species seem actually to compose with these variations using the sonata form found in classical music. A song sparrow will belt out a theme much like an opening of a classical piece. It then improvises here and there, just as a human composer develops a theme before rambling back to the final recapitulation.

Many Floridians have favorite stories of hearing a car alarm or camera click and suddenly realizing it's a mockingbird perched on a bush. The current theory for such mimicry is based on the fact that female songbirds often prefer males with larger song repertoires, so they select males that can sing twenty song variants over males that sing only ten. In mockingbirds and other mimics, this process has expanded to the point that birds now have the capacity to incorporate other sounds. Could this be a new tool for music schools?

If you want to improve your ability to "bird by ear," pick up the very good tape of birdcalls entitled *Sounds of Florida's Birds* by John William Hardy, available at many nature shops across Florida. In addition to calls and songs, the tape also includes information on where birds breed and when you can expect to hear them, a valuable addition to any compendium of songs. When you buy this tape (or some other recording), also purchase a blank, much shorter tape that holds just three minutes on each side. This will enable you to copy a subset of the songs found on the longer tape to the shorter tape, and work more diligently with the shorter tape. It can be quite intimidating—and boring—trying to learn calls by starting at common loon and listening straight through, all the way to house finch. Transfer songs of ten birds at a time to the shorter tape and work with these. Begin with the common birds around your house—mockingbirds, cardinals, brown thrashers—and once you have learned these, put a new group of songs on the shorter tape. You will soon be on your way to the seemingly mysterious realm of identification by song.

Teal Cluster

79. Fox Lake Park   114

80. Blue Heron Wetlands Treatment Facility   114

81. Kennedy Point Park   115

82. Pine Island Conservation Area   116

83. J. G. Bourbeau Park   116

84. Kelly Park   117

85. Port's End Park   117

86. Jetty Maritime Park   118

87. Rotary Park at Merritt Island   119

88. Lori Wilson Park   119

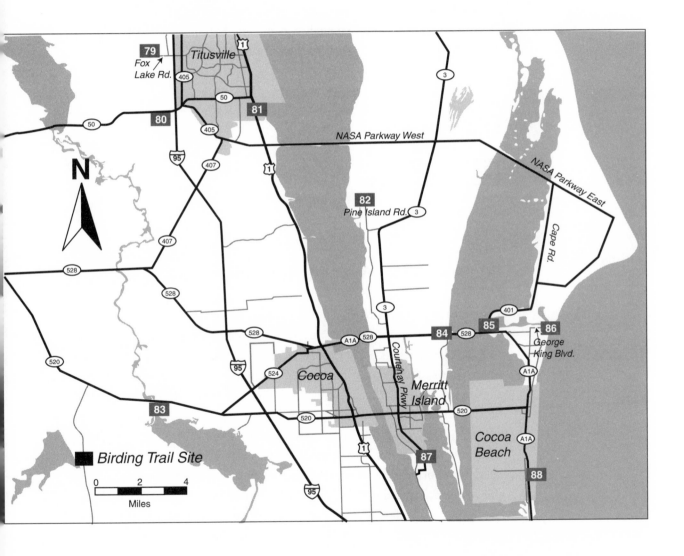

79. Fox Lake Park

DESCRIPTION: Fox Lake offers a variety of water and wading birds such as coots, snowy egrets, green herons, and anhingas. Eurasian collared doves feed in the open park spaces, and the occasional raptor feeds on the Eurasian collared doves! Migrant songbirds like pine warblers can be found in the oaks and along the forest edges. The lake can be further explored by kayak (bring your own), yielding up treats such as swallow-tailed kites, limpkins, and roseate spoonbills. Trails to the east are planned to provide access to the St. Johns River National Wildlife Refuge.

DIRECTIONS: From the intersection of SR 50 and SR 405 in Titusville, take 405 (South Street) north approximately two and one-half miles to Fox Lake Road. Turn left (west) and go two miles to the site at the end.

Open sunrise to sunset. Best months for birding are January–December.

(321) 264-5105.

www.brevardparks.com.

80. Blue Heron Wetlands Treatment Facility

DESCRIPTION: A created wetland, Blue Heron not only polishes reclaimed water for the city of Titusville but is also home to an amazing diversity of wetland bird species. One of the first facilities of its kind in the country, it uses water plants to absorb nutrients like phosphates and nitrates that remain in the highly treated effluent water. This helps prevent river-choking algae blooms in the stream into which the water is discharged. Wading birds are common here year-round, as are purple gallinules and both bitterns. Shorebirds and ducks winter in the impoundments from late October through February, and northern harriers patrol the marshes in search of a meal (watch for piles of feathers on the dikes, indicating a raptor with a full stomach). Dikes are open to vehicular traffic, and are exposed, so bring sunscreen and beware of summer lightning storms. Be sure to sign in and out of the facility at the office.

DIRECTIONS: From Titusville, take SR 50 west. Turn left (south) on Deep Marsh Road approximately half a mile past I-95. The site is at the end of the road. If the gate is closed, ring the buzzer. Sign in at the first building on the left.

Open dawn to dusk. Sign-in and -out at office required. Best months for birding are January–December.

(321) 383-5642.

81. Kennedy Point Park

DESCRIPTION: Scoping for wintering ducks, loons, and grebes is often a matter of luck; the more spots you check, the more likely you are to find them. Kennedy Point is worth a visit to scan the Indian River for these winter waterbirds. Check for laughing, ring-billed, and herring gulls along the seawall. Ruddy turnstones frequently race around the rocks and neighboring docks also. Riverfront Park half a mile north of Kennedy Point offers similar opportunities. Turnstones, gulls, and terns are all likely there. These are highly seasonal sites, best in fall and winter.

DIRECTIONS: From Titusville, travel a quarter mile south on US 1 from SR 50. The park is on the left (east) side of the road.

Open sunrise to sunset. Best months for birding are October–February.

(321) 264-5105.

www.brevardparks.com

82. Pine Island Conservation Area

DESCRIPTION: Pine Island offers another good look at migratory ducks like blue-winged teal and American wigeon, with blinds on several of the interior ponds. A pine flatwoods on the west side of the property attracts migratory songbirds, and the open marsh harbors wading birds and shorebirds. Duck hunts occur on the north part of the property two days a month, November through January. During hunts, the check station at the entrance will notify you that the north part of the property is closed to birdwatching. Get a map at the entrance kiosk, and if you're so inclined, consider bringing a canoe or kayak. These can be launched in the series of ponds at the north and south ends of the property and can be navigated out into the lagoon, returning up the coast to the launch again. This property is part of Brevard County's innovative Environmentally Endangered Lands program.

DIRECTIONS: From the intersection on Merritt Island with SR 528, take North Courtenay Parkway (SR 3) north five miles to Pine Island Road. Turn left (west)and follow Pine Island Road two and one-half miles to the parking lot at the end.

Open 7:00 A.M. to sunset. Best months for birding are October–April.

(321) 633-2046.

www.eelbrevard.com.

83. J. G. Bourbeau Park

DESCRIPTION: James G. Bourbeau Memorial Park on the broad St. Johns River floodplain provides a vantage of the river for waders like wood storks, migratory ducks in fall and winter, and shorebirds like black-necked stilts. Limpkins are likely, and crested caracaras and snail kites have been seen occasionally from this location. Bird the park's waterfront, but also check the gravel boat launch area across the road for a different, quieter view. This site gets heavy boat traffic on weekends, so it is best visited during the week.

DIRECTIONS: From Cocoa, take SR 520 west. Approximately five miles after I-95, the park is on the east side of the St. Johns River bridge, on the south side of the road.

Open sunrise to sunset. Best months for birding are October–April.

(321) 633-1874.

www.brevardparks.com.

84. Kelly Park

DESCRIPTION: Kelly Park on the Banana River provides a good view of the river, where you may see rafts of ducks like green-winged teal, common and red-throated loons, and horned grebes in fall and winter. Shorebirds such as spotted sandpipers and wading birds can be seen on exposed shoals at low tide. Check the mudflats on the north side of the causeway for additional species. Blue herons have been known to nest in the tops of neighboring pine trees, but otherwise the site is much better in fall and winter than in summer.

DIRECTIONS: On Merritt Island, take SR 528 east and exit on North Banana River Drive. Kelly Park is south of SR 528 on the west side of the Banana River.

Open sunrise to sunset. Best months for birding are October–April.

(321) 633-1874.

www.brevardparks.com.

85. Port's End Park

DESCRIPTION: Port's End is worth a visit if you're already out by Port Canaveral—check the lock area, on the rocks, for shorebirds like ruddy turnstones and spotted sandpipers. Brown pelicans and double-crested cormorants loaf on the sea wall, along with great blue herons and snowy egrets.

Directions: Take SR 528 east toward Port Canaveral and choose the "B" side (south) entrance into the port. Turn left onto Mullet Drive. Port's End Park is located before the drawbridge on the right. Canaveral Locks are at the very end of Mullet Drive.

Open sunrise to sunset. Best months for birding are January–December.

(321) 783-7831.

www.portcanaveral.org.

86. Jetty Maritime Park

Description: The jetty of Jetty Maritime Park is the last land ships pass as they leave Port Canaveral, headed out to sea. From the north end of the park, check the ship turning basin from the jetty. The turning basin is known for uncommon ducks in the fall and winter and, regardless, will have loons, cormorants, and mergansers during those months. Beach birds such as ruddy turnstones and willets are common; large flocks of terns, black skimmers, and gulls also loaf on the beach. Pelagics such as gannets may be seen with a scope from the jetty. A small hammock on-site can be good for songbirds during migration.

Directions: Take SR 528 east toward Port Canaveral. When approaching the port facility, take the "B" side (south) entrance and follow George King Boulevard east to Jetty Park.

Open 7:00 A.M. to 10:00 P.M. Best months for birding are October–March.

(321) 783-7111.

87. Rotary Park at Merritt Island

DESCRIPTION: Primarily good for migratory songbirds in season, Rotary Park has an elevated boardwalk through a hardwood hammock. Its nature center is open by appointment for groups.

DIRECTIONS: Take SR 520 onto Merritt Island. Turn right (south) on Courtenay Parkway and travel two and a half miles to the park entrance on the right (west) side of the road.

Open sunrise to sunset. Best months for birding are October–April.

(321) 455-1385.

www.brevardparks.com.

88. Lori Wilson Park

DESCRIPTION: Lori Wilson Park has examples of maritime hammock, excellent for migratory songbirds and painted buntings, and coastal scrub for Florida scrub-jays, as well as beach access for shorebirds and seabirds. Springtime songbird migration fallouts occur in April and can garner day lists of about fifteen warbler species. Additionally, the park's on-site nature center provides an opportunity to learn how habitats like maritime hammock and coastal scrub are struggling to survive with continued coastal development.

DIRECTIONS: From SR 520 in Cocoa Beach, take SR A1A three and a half miles south. The park is on the left (east) side of the road.

Open sunrise to sunset; nature center hours vary. Best months for birding are January–December.

(321) 633-1874.

www.brevardparks.com.

When Birds Can't Rise Above the Fray

Jim Cox

Florida's red-light districts are growing. Scan the horizon as you ride a dark road and you will see scores of small red lights—some blinking, some not—rising above the trees on tall steel towers.

The lights are not meant to lure someone to the seedy side of town, but rather to warn air travelers of danger nearby. Unfortunately, this warning works only for a handful of the air travelers using Florida's skies.

Communication towers help us reach out and touch someone, but these and other tall structures also can stop many migratory songbirds dead in their tracks. Most songbirds migrate at night, and on clear nights they have little trouble seeing and steering clear of tall structures. But when bad weather in the form of fog or low clouds sets in and visibility is limited, birds strike towers and buildings and fall to the ground in big numbers.

One of the best studies of this comes from a thousand-foot tower that stood just north of Tallahassee until the mid-1980s. For twenty-five years, ornithologists scoured the field beneath this tower and gathered birds killed the previous night. They picked up more than 42,000 birds representing 190 species, and on particularly bad nights, as many as 2,000 birds could be found scattered beneath the tower. They also estimated that another 4,000 to 6,000 might have been killed and then carted off by scavengers before being counted. Fall migration is generally the worst tower kill season, as millions of songbirds stream over Florida.

Observers of severe tower kills describe birds swirling around the towers in a deadly dance. The flashing lights reflect off the water in the air and form a halo of light that disorients the birds, which circle until they collide with guy wires, the tower, or other birds—or the fog clears.

The killing capacity of a tower depends on its height, location, guy wires, and other variables, and there are few hard data from all the types of towers that exist. Although precise estimates for the number killed each year are difficult to come by, some place the number around 4 or 5 million. Others think as many as 20 million songbirds die this way.

In the late 1960s, when the number of towers was a small fraction of what it is today, tower kills accounted for much less than one percent of the total annual mortality of most birds. This percentage is likely increasing. According to the Federal Aviation Administration, there are now more than 60,000 communication towers across the United States, and an estimated 5,000 new towers are being built each year. As digital television becomes more commonplace, estimates are that as many as a thousand new tall TV towers (the most deadly, for sure) could be built across the country over the next decade.

Studies are needed to document the cumulative impact of towers, but some worry that a dozen or so migratory species already experiencing declines may be greatly affected by towers. So listen very carefully if you use a cell phone or have the radio operating on a rainy fall night. The static you hear may be more than meets the ears.

Gateway to the Great Florida Birding Trail

Tenoroc Fish Management Area

Jenny Novak

When people think of phosphate mining, they think of barren "moon-scapes." Phosphate ore has been strip-mined in Florida since the early 1890s and continues to be mined today. Active mines have little wildlife value and do resemble the moon in appearance, but, given time, nature can work wonders in the ecological recovery of these man-made land-scapes. One such wonderland is the Tenoroc Fish Management Area.

About two miles northeast of Lakeland lies Tenoroc. This mostly un-known expanse of mined land is a haven for songbirds, raptors, and wad-ing birds. Coronet Industries began mining here in the 1950s; twenty years later Tenoroc (Coronet spelled backwards) was sold to Borden, Inc. Bor-den continued to mine, but donated the property to the State of Florida in 1983, opening the door for public use of this hidden jewel. For several years the Department of Natural Resources held the lease to Tenoroc, but in 1993 the Florida Fish and Wildlife Conservation Commission took over the property with a vision for the future.

Tenoroc is situated at the headwaters of the Peace River, and links that river to its source, the Green Swamp. Waters routed from the swamp through the pit lakes have kept them healthy and refreshed and allowed vegetation to come back naturally. Over time, a continuous greenway has become established that now serves as an important refuge for migrating birds. Tenoroc's lakes are teeming with forage and sport fish, a desirable condition for both human and nonhuman anglers. By controlling the numbers of human anglers and their harvest, and through restricted use of boat motors, Tenoroc has been able to provide quality sport fishing opportunities for the public while maintaining one of the state's largest wading bird rookeries. These and other noninvasive management approaches have resulted in a myriad of habitats that support a diversity of bird species, many of which are year-round residents. So it is easy to say, anytime is a good time to go birding at Tenoroc!

Throughout the year lakes and wetlands are filled with a variety of bird life. Common to the terrain are great and little blue herons and great and snowy egrets. Look for these keen hunters stalking the lakes' edges, as well as white ibises and sandhill cranes. Also making the occasional appearance are least bitterns, glossy ibises, tricolored herons, and green herons. Scan the shores for common moorhens and limpkins, and watch the water for wood ducks and Florida mallards. In winter, white pelicans soar gracefully along while belted kingfishers patiently watch for their next meal. In summer, lucky birders can catch glimpses of black-necked stilts and least terns.

Raptors build their nests in the trees and hunt over water or field at Tenoroc. There are always osprey, red-shouldered hawks, and black and turkey vultures in the neighborhood. Bald eagles have been spotted, and in summer the swallow-tailed kites arrive. Winter is the time to see American kestrels, northern harriers, and peregrine falcons.

Throughout the seasons, Tenoroc's trees and fields and marshes are filled with the calls and songs of pileated woodpeckers, white-eyed vireos, eastern meadowlarks, and red-winged blackbirds. For songbirds, fall is the best time of the year, when a host of transient species stop in on their migratory voyages. Avid birders will want to look for Acadian flycatchers, American redstarts, prothonotary warblers, and blue-winged warblers, and an autumn walk in the woods may be rewarded with the silvery, fluted song of the veery.

Purple Gallinule Cluster

89. Tenoroc Fish
Management
Area   125

90. Saddle Creek
Park   126

91. Lake Hollings-
worth   126

92. Peace River Park
127

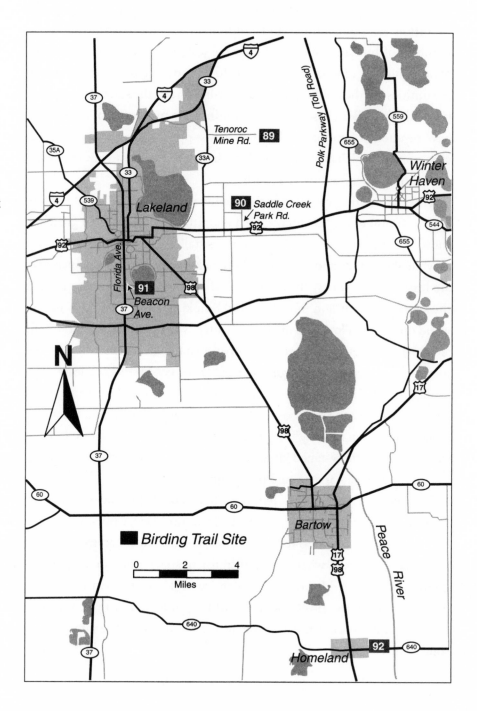

89. Tenoroc Fish Management Area

Description: Tenoroc is a gateway for the East Section of the Great Florida Birding Trail, acting as a source of information about the Birding Trail and birding activities in this eighteen-county area. Check the entrance kiosk for information about the Trail, and check in at the office to pay your entrance fee and pick up a map of the area. Loaner binoculars are available if you've forgotten your own. This large area has a variety of habitats suitable for birding. Drive down to Picnic Lake, watching along the way for meadowlarks and raptors in the grasslands. At Picnic Lake watch for birds wading in the lake, and hike the trail around Cemetery Lake looking for migratory ducks like blue-winged teal and hooded mergansers. Northern harriers are common in winter, and by hiking the dike trail across the road from Picnic Lake's parking area, you can reach an area overlooking a wading bird colony featuring snowy egrets, white ibises, and anhingas in the springtime. South of the office, follow the dirt road to the dove field, which can be good for sparrows (this area is closed during dove season). By hiking further south, you can reach an unmined portion of the property with an impressive list of migratory songbirds from August to October and again in April. This area is rugged, so take water and be sure to pick up a map at the office. Remember to check out at the office when you leave.

Directions: From I-4 east of Lakeland, take SR 33 south 1.4 miles to SR 33A. Veer left on Combee Road (SR 33A) and follow it 1.2 miles to Tenoroc Mine Road. Turn left (west) and proceed to the Tenoroc Fish Management Area office on the right.

Open for birding Friday through Monday, 6:00 A.M. to 5:30 P.M.; office open weekdays, 8:00 A.M. to 5:00 P.M. Best months for birding are September–May.

(863) 499-2421 Tuesday through Thursday, (863) 499-2422 Friday through Monday.

http://floridaconservation.org/fishing/offices/tenoroc-home.

90. Saddle Creek Park

DESCRIPTION: On the drive in, watch the wetlands for wading birds like glossy ibis and limpkin. At first blush Saddle Creek Park looks like it must be best known for its wading birds, but in truth it is one of Florida's premier warbler locations during migration. Drive to the north end of the park and leave your car by the maintenance shed at the trailhead parking lot. Hiking the trail through the mixed hardwood and cypress forest, you stand the chance of seeing Saddle Creek's whopping twenty-two recorded warbler species in the fall migration from August through October and again in April. Lake Region Audubon leads bird walks every Saturday from August through September around 7:30 A.M. Call their Street Nature Center for details (see site 93). Saddle Creek Park has no maps available, but the trails are very well marked and there should be little concern about getting lost. The ability to bird by ear helps tremendously, although you should get some good sightings here too.

DIRECTIONS: Take US 92 east from Lakeland to Saddle Creek Park Road. Turn left (north) to enter the park.

Open 5:00 A.M. to 10:00 P.M. Best months for birding are August–April.

(863) 534-4340.

www.polk-county.net.

91. Lake Hollingsworth

DESCRIPTION: The urban Lake Hollingsworth in the middle of Lakeland has a remarkable diversity of wading birds and easy viewing opportunities. A sidewalk trail runs three miles around the lake and can be walked, biked, or rollerbladed. Purple gallinules are common on the south-southeast corner of the lake and are very habituated to people, so you can get a very close look—great for photographers. Wading birds like the great egret, snowy egret, great blue heron, and tricolored heron are common too. Watch the cattails for black-crowned night herons and least bittern, and in winter there will be least, royal, and Caspian terns plunging for fish in the lake. During periods of low water, avocets and sandpipers have been seen, and black-necked stilts are common in winter and early spring. Wood storks frequent the west side of the lake, and great blue herons often nest in the oaks on the lake's edge. Watch the trees for migrants like cedar waxwings in season. White pelicans feed in flocks on the lake in winter. This lake is an "eye candy" birding spot, a delight for beginners and experts alike. Water fountains are located every mile along the route, but do remember that the trail is in full sun for most of its three-mile length. Lake Morton, one mile north of Lake Hollingsworth, has wintering ring-necked ducks as well.

DIRECTIONS: From I-4, take Florida Avenue (SR 98) south into Lakeland. Pass through downtown and turn left (east) on Beacon Avenue. The road dead-ends on Lake Hollingsworth Drive. Turn right, proceed through one traffic light, and park in the public parking on the left (north) side of the road. You are at the southernmost point on the lake.

Open sunrise to sunset. Best months for birding are January–December.

City of Lakeland: (863) 834-6040.

www.government.lakeland.net.

92. Peace River Park

DESCRIPTION: Peace River Park offers a boardwalk through the cypress flood-plain forest down to the river itself. Winding through ancient trees and the cool shade of swampland, the boardwalk takes you through a migrant song-bird mecca, and where it ends at the river, you will likely see wading birds and migratory ducks. Duck species seen include green-winged and blue-winged teal, American wigeon, ring-necked duck, lesser scaup, hooded merganser, and ruddy duck. This site's bird list includes three thrush, four vireo, and twenty-two warbler species. Knowing your birdcalls helps in this forest; its high canopy makes viewing difficult at times, although sound carries, so calls are clear.

DIRECTIONS: From Bartow, take SR 98 south to Homeland. Turn left (east) on CR 640. There are two park entrances on the north side of CR 640, approximately one mile apart. The boardwalk entrance is the easternmost of the two.

Open 5:00 A.M. to 10:00 P.M. Best months for birding are March–May, September–November.

(863) 534-4340.

Birding the Lake Wales Ridge

Tom Palmer

If you need a good reason to visit the Lake Wales Ridge, start with Florida scrub-jays, the only bird species found only in Florida. These birds live on the remaining undeveloped scrub islands that form the state's topographic spine. Call them the High Tortugas, the place where gopher tortoises instead of loggerhead turtles help to define the sense of place. These ridges, remnants of ancient sand dunes, are home to many threatened and endangered plants and animals. Because this high ground is coveted for use as homesites and orange groves, the natural areas remaining on the ridge are that much more special—for people and birds alike.

Whether you visit Lake Kissimmee State Park east of Lake Wales (site 95), Highlands Hammock State Park at the edge of Sebring (site 122) or Lake Wales Ridge State Forest outside of Frostproof (sites 99 and 100), you'll find scrub-jays and much more. Hundreds of species of birds nest here, winter here, or just pass through during migration. The lakes that dot and surround the Lake Wales Ridge make it one of the best places in Florida to see bald eagles: seeing ten a day or ten at a time is not unheard of. This is also a place where you're likely to see an elegant swallow-tailed kite gliding over the early summer treetops. If you're lucky, a short-tailed hawk may appear from nowhere against the clouds. I've seen short-tailed hawks regularly along the Peace River and Saddle Creek, also good places to find migrating songbirds, especially in the fall. Saddle Creek Park near Lakeland (one of the most dependable places to find limpkins; see site 90) is best, but Peace River Park south of Bartow (site 92) can also be productive.

One thing that makes the ridge so attractive to birdwatchers is the mosaic of habitats. In places east of Lake Wales, you could be standing on white sand looking at a red-headed or a hairy woodpecker in a pine tree, and then walk fifty yards down to the creek and hear a parula warbler or a red-eyed vireo singing, or flush a pair of wood ducks.

At sites on the ridge, you can see a flock of wild turkeys running through the oak hammocks, or watch sandhill cranes in roadside pastures. Sandhills nest here, but the area also attracts large flocks of migrating cranes from elsewhere in North America. Many of those migrating cranes congregate in the retention ponds at Eagle Ridge Mall (site 94).

The activity at the retention ponds is a reminder not to confine your bird trips to looking for land birds. The shallow marshes that dot the Lake Wales Ridge attract shorebirds of all types—yellowlegs, sandpipers, dowitchers, snipe—and waders that don't wade much, such as ibises. The area is a good place to see glossy ibis, a species that was once uncommon locally. On the lakes, common moorhens, coots, egrets, and herons are a given; mixed flocks of wintering waterfowl are a bonus. Sometimes it isn't the species but the numbers that are impressive. I've seen lakes with hundreds of pied-billed grebes along with the wigeon and ringnecks. Scan the lakes carefully. Common loons and horned grebes are likely in the cleaner lakes, but I've also seen bufflehead and eared grebes. And don't just scan the open water, scan the edges too. Snail kites have been showing up in unexpected places.

When you visit the Lake Wales Ridge, always be alert for an odd bird in an odd place. After all, it was a pair of tourists who found a northern lapwing in a pasture in Highlands County in 1997—and a new state record.

If you're planning to visit the Lake Wales Ridge, a good local source to visit first is the Polk County bird website assembled by veteran local birdwatcher Chuck Geanangel. The address is www.angelfire.com/fl2/polkcountybirds/.

Ridge Cluster

93. Lake Region Audubon's Street Nature Center   131

94. Eagle Ridge Mall   131

95. Lake Kissimmee State Park   132

96. Bok Tower Gardens   132

97. Lake Wailes   133

98. Ridge Audubon Nature Center   134

99. Lake Wales Ridge State Forest: Walk-in-the-Water Tract   134

100. Lake Wales Ridge State Forest: Arbuckle Tract   135

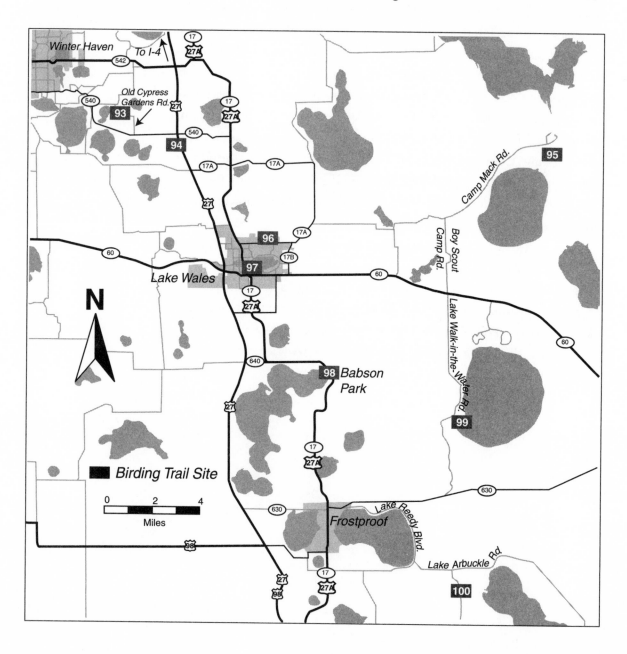

93. Street Nature Center

DESCRIPTION: Street Nature Center is owned and operated by the Lake Region Audubon Society. Offering trails through hardwood forest down to a lakefront, the area is excellent for migrants like indigo buntings. Resident limpkins and bald eagles are likely on the waterfront, and the site's migrating warbler list tops twenty species. A demonstration butterfly garden and interpretive trail add educational value to the site. The Center also offers a variety of educational programs, as well as off-site field trips to migration hot spots like Saddle Creek Park. Call in advance for details and reservations, or check their website, which is updated regularly.

DIRECTIONS: From US 27 north of Lake Wales, take Cypress Gardens Boulevard (CR 540) west to the intersection with Old Cypress Gardens Road. Turn north on Old Cypress Gardens Road and follow it through a turn to the west. After this turn, look for Lameraux Road on the right (north). Street Nature Center is at 115 Lameraux Road on the left. Park in the lot at the end of the dirt entrance road.

Open 8:00 A.M. to 5:00 P.M. Best months for birding are September–April.

(863) 324-7304.

www.lakeregion.net.

94. Eagle Ridge Mall

DESCRIPTION: "You want me to bird WHERE??" That's right—the Eagle Ridge Mall has surprisingly good birding in the retention pond on its north side. In fall, winter, and early spring, it is chock full of shorebirds ranging from dunlin to snipe to spotted sandpipers. An excellent site to add shorebirds to your day list in landlocked Polk County, it is easily accessible from I-4, and if you're lucky, you may even catch a northern harrier stalking the shorebirds while you're there! Park in the lot and walk to the grassy edge of the pond. Be sure to stand clear of the road to avoid passing mall traffic. Sandhill cranes roost here in the evenings, and waders and bitterns frequent the pond too. This is a little-known yet well-accepted site among Florida birders.

DIRECTIONS: The Eagle Ridge Mall is located on the east side of US 27, five miles north of Lake Wales and seventeen miles south of I-4.

Open sunrise to sunset. Best months for birding are October–April.

(863) 676-2300.

95. Lake Kissimmee State Park

DESCRIPTION: The fabulous Lake Kissimmee State Park is teeming with birdlife. On the drive in, watch for crested caracaras, bald eagles, turkeys, and bobwhite. The entrance station is a good spot to check for scrub-jays, and then the possibilities are endless. Watch for red-headed woodpeckers in flatwoods as you drive in, and hike to the overlook at the picnic area. You can walk all the way to the lake watching for waders and looking for snail kites, take a guided boat tour, or rent a canoe and explore the water for yourself. The cow camp area across the bridge from the picnic area is excellent for songbird migrants, and occasionally the marsh edges of the lake will host a whooping crane or two. Come prepared to hike, and bring water, a hat, and lunch. Camping is available at this property too, and would give you access to the area at night to prowl for owls and other nocturnal specialties. Summers are hot and buggy, so be prepared.

DIRECTIONS: From the intersection of US 27 and SR 60 in Lake Wales, take SR 60 east nine miles to Boy Scout Camp Road. Turn left (north) and proceed to Camp Mack Road. Turn right (east) and follow Camp Mack Road to the park entrance.

Open 7:00 A.M. to sunset. Best months for birding are October–May.

(863) 696-1112.

www.dep.state.fl.us/parks.

96. Bok Tower Gardens

DESCRIPTION: A cultivated garden, Bok Tower Gardens also has a native landscape in which you can find birds like kestrels, nighthawks, pileated woodpeckers, and loggerhead shrikes. Check the cultivated gardens for hummingbirds in spring and summer, as well as migratory songbirds during September and October and again in April. This organization has made significant contributions to the conservation of rare plants on the Lake Wales Ridge and offers excellent educational opportunities about the ridge's endangered upland habitats and their bird inhabitants. Bok Tower Gardens also coordinates off-site birding field trips, so call in advance for details and reservations for your group.

DIRECTIONS: From US 27 north of SR 60, exit east onto Mountain Lake Cut-off Road and go to US 17/27A. Turn right on 17 (south) and go about half a mile to Burns Avenue. Turn left (east) and go to the top of the hill; the entrance to Bok Tower Gardens will be on the left (north) side of the road.

Open 8:00 A.M. to 6:00 P.M.; last admission, 5:00 P.M. Best months for birding are October–April.

(863) 676-1408.

www.boktowergardens.org.

97. Lake Wailes

DESCRIPTION: Lake Wailes (the lake) is worth a quick stop if you're in the area of Lake Wales (the town). Drive to the northwest corner of the lake and park your car. Bird the oaks for migrants in season including kinglets and warblers, and look at the lake for waders, anhingas, sandhill cranes, and wintering duck species. A path leads around the lake clockwise from the southwest corner to a park on the northeast corner. Walk the trail for more extensive looks at the lake.

DIRECTIONS: On US 27 just north of SR 60 in Lake Wales, turn east onto Central Avenue and proceed until it dead-ends at the lake. There are two parking sites on the northwest and north sides of the lake.

Open sunrise to sunset. Best months for birding are October–April.

(863) 678-4182.

www.cityoflakewales.com.

98. Ridge Audubon Nature Center

DESCRIPTION: The nature center run by the Ridge Audubon Society is a good educational resource for birding, bird conservation, and upland conservation. Babson Park lies on the Lake Wales Ridge, an elevated backbone that runs down the middle of central Florida and supports some of the most unique and threatened uplands in Florida. Visit this informative site to learn more about Florida's endangered uplands and their inhabitants; walk their nature trail to see a sandhill in person, watching for its birds like eastern towhees, white-eyed vireos, ground doves, and nighthawks.

DIRECTIONS: From the intersection of US 27 and SR 60 in Lake Wales, take US 27 south four miles to CR 640. Turn left (east). CR 640 will join SR 17 as it turns south. The nature center will be on the southwest corner of the intersection with North Crooked Lake Drive in Babson Park.

Open Tuesday through Saturday, 9:30 A.M. to 2:30 P.M. Trails open dawn to dusk. Best months for birding are January–December.

(863) 638-1355.

E-mail: Raudubon@cs.com.

99. Lake Wales Ridge State Forest: Walk-in-the-Water Tract

DESCRIPTION: Walk-in-the-Water is rustic, and best for a few sought-after species. The main entrance at King Trail Gate is a good location for Florida scrub-jays, as well as flyovers by short-tailed hawks. The hawks nest nearby and can be seen frequently in this area. The other trails, Long Pond and Big Bay, wind through scrub appropriate for Florida scrub-jays and eastern towhees, with occasional wetland pockets good for migratory songbirds. This property is beautiful but has very little signage and directional information. Be sure to take water, a hat, and a map with you before hiking far into its interior. There are some limited hunts on this property; call in advance for dates.

DIRECTIONS: From Lake Wales, take SR 60 east approximately seven miles to Walk-in-the-Water Road. Turn right (south) and go approximately five miles. Entrances to the forest will be on the right side of the road.

Open sunrise to sunset. Best months for birding are October–April.

(863) 635-7801.

www.fl-dof.com.

100. Lake Wales Ridge State Forest: Arbuckle Tract

DESCRIPTION: As you drive into the Arbuckle Tract, watch for scrub-jays on either side of the road in areas of five-foot-tall oak scrub. Stop at the entrance kiosk to pick up a map and a bird list, and proceed to one of the several trailheads lining the road. On the left side, trailheads lead through migratory songbird habitat down to Lake Arbuckle, where you can see wading birds and bald eagles, limpkins and migratory ducks. The Reedy Creek Trail offers a chance for short-tailed hawks, and the Lake Godwin flatwoods are a good location for brown-headed nuthatches. This area has several hunting seasons, so call ahead for dates or check at the office before you begin your hikes. Take water and a map to hike these trails. Summer is very hot and buggy.

DIRECTIONS: From Lake Wales, take US 27 south ten miles to CR 630A. Go east four miles, through Frostproof, to Lake Reedy Boulevard and turn right (southeast). Follow Lake Reedy Boulevard three miles to Lake Arbuckle Road and turn left (east). The forest entrance will be approximately one mile on your right. Roads are dirt, but safe for two-wheel-drive vehicles.

Open sunrise to sunset. Best months for birding are October–April.

(863) 635-7801.

www.fl-dof.com.

Whooping Cranes Return to Florida

Steve Nesbitt

My nine-year-old son and I huddled in a blind on central Florida's Kissimmee Prairie, watching five whooping cranes feeding. For more than twenty-one years I had spent countless hours watching and studying thousands of sandhill cranes in Florida, pleasurable labors that now enabled me to watch these five whooping cranes explore their new home. After an absence of seventy-six years, this magnificent endangered crane had returned to Florida.

As we watched, I thought of my grandfather, Ira Gabrielson, who stimulated my interest in the outdoors and started me on a career in biology. One of the last to see whooping cranes in his home state of Iowa, he went on to become a professional ornithologist and served as the director of the United States Biological Survey/Fish and Wildlife Service from 1935 to 1946. It was during this time that the Aransas National Wildlife Refuge was created on the Texas coast, signaling the start of a slow but steady comeback for the endangered whooping crane, the tallest bird in North America. Whooping crane numbers had declined from 500–700 individuals in 1870 to a low of twenty-two in 1941. In 1939 my grandfather helped establish the Patuxent Wildlife Research Center, today the largest of three breeding centers for whooping cranes. As I watched the birds feeding, I wondered if he could have imagined the enormous effort that has gone into reversing the whooping crane's slide toward extinction.

This effort includes a plan to restore populations of whooping cranes in selected areas of their former range in the southeastern United States. Today, only one wild population of whooping cranes remains in North America, spending winters at Aransas NWR and migrating each spring to nest in the bogs of the Northwest Territories of Canada. Historically, whooping cranes also bred around the Great Lakes, and some wintered along the southeastern Atlantic Coast, including Florida. One of the last of this population was shot in St. Johns County in 1927 or 1928.

After a decade of research, the Whooping Crane Recovery Team recommended that a nonmigratory flock be established on the Kissimmee Prairie in Florida. Accordingly, the first release of whooping cranes occurred in February 1993. The five birds my son and I watched would be the first of 208 young birds released to date on these prairies. More than 80 of these whooping cranes survive in Florida today. Bobcat predation and other natural causes have claimed the rest.

In 1999, reintroduced whooping cranes laid eggs in Florida for the first time, and in the spring of 2000 a pair of whooping cranes hatched the first eggs in the wild in the United States in sixty years! One of those chicks died of unknown causes, and a second was near fledging before a bobcat killed it. Yet in spite of the loss, the 2000 season was a resounding success. A pair of whooping cranes, born in captivity and released into the wild, had successfully reproduced and cared for a growing chick. We now knew that whooping cranes would do what we had so long hoped: reproduce their kind in a natural Florida habitat.

My grandfather died never expecting that whooping cranes would one day forage for crayfish, frogs, and snakes alongside sandhill cranes on a Florida prairie. Yet his great-grandson and others who care to look will likely see these striking white birds become an accepted sight on the Florida landscape.

Whooping Crane Cluster

101. Forever Florida
139

102. Joe Overstreet
Landing   139

103. Three Lakes
Wildlife Man-
agement Area
140

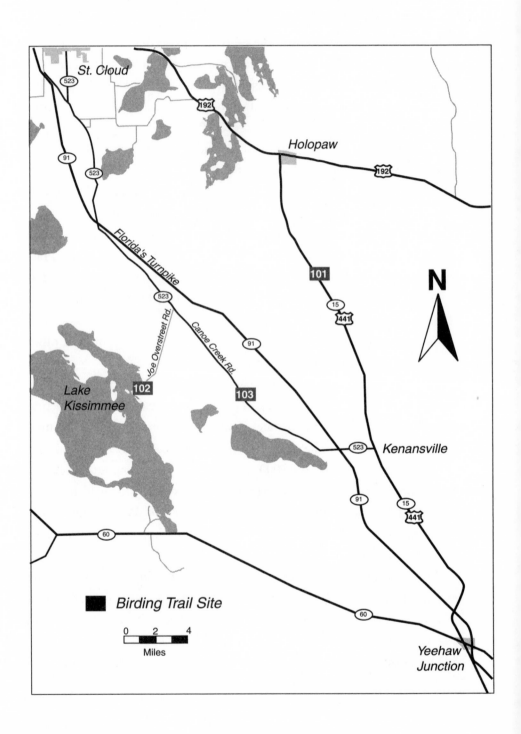

101. Forever Florida

DESCRIPTION: A privately owned tour covers the Crescent J cattle ranch as well as untouched flatwoods, prairies, and hammocks of the adjacent Forever Florida Preserve. Tours are by a four-wheel-drive, open-air elevated coach, from which you can see massive flocks of turkeys, soaring bald eagles, and sandhill cranes nesting in seasonal ponds. Explore the hammock of Bull Creek, listening for migratory songbirds and watching for resident wading birds. Call in advance for details; the visitor center and restaurant are open 8:00 A.M. to 9:00 P.M. This site offers a great opportunity to learn more about Florida's habitats and how many are managed with fire for the health of all their inhabitants.

DIRECTIONS: From St. Cloud, take US 192 east to US 441. Turn right (south) and go seven and one-half miles. Forever Florida will be on the left (east) side of the road.

Visitor center open 8:00 A.M. to 9:00 P.M. Best months for birding are October–April.

(888) 957-9794.

www.foreverflorida.com.

102. Joe Overstreet Landing

DESCRIPTION: As you drive down Joe Overstreet Road, look carefully in the pastures on either side for whooping cranes. They are part of a reintroduction project to establish a nonmigratory flock here in Florida. The flock is still very small, so this location is probably your best chance to see a whooper in Florida. Also, watch the pastures for sandhill cranes and turkeys, and the fence posts for meadowlarks, bald eagles, and crested caracaras. At the end of the road, check the boat ramp area for limpkins and other waders, and snail kites, and scope the lake for ducks. Overstreet Road is fairly rural, so you can feel comfortable pulling over for a better look. Please respect private property, however, and stay on the road, the right-of-way, and the public boat ramp area at the end of the road.

DIRECTIONS: From St. Cloud, take Vermont Avenue, which becomes Canoe Creek Road (CR 523), south twenty miles to Joe Overstreet Road. Turn right (southwest) and follow the road to the boat ramp at the end.

Open sunrise to sunset. Best months for birding are January–December.

103. Three Lakes Wildlife Management Area

Description: The Three Lakes area, long known for its excellent hunting opportunities, has also been a favorite of birders. Recently the Florida Fish and Wildlife Conservation Commission designed and installed an educational driving loop through the property, from which birding can be excellent. Start at the entrance to the Prairie Lakes Unit, where you can pick up a map, pay your honor fee, and break out your binoculars. The driving loop runs five miles across sloughs and through flatwoods, oak hammocks, and scrubby areas. Watch along the ecotones—where one habitat meets another—since these are often the most productive areas for birding. Feeding guilds, or groups of different birds feeding together, move through the oaks and pines in winter, and the drive goes right past a cluster of red-cockaded woodpecker nest trees before the exit from the wildlife drive. Turkeys, wood storks, and limpkins are common in the area. Of course, getting out and hiking will make for more productive birding. Be aware that this is a fairly wild area—take water, a map, and a compass—and also check the kiosks at the entrances to see if hunts occur during your visit. In the westernmost portion of the Prairie Lakes Unit, grasshopper, Bachman's, Henslow's, and savannah sparrows can be found, as well as occasional short-tailed hawks. White-tailed kites have also been known to breed in this wildlife management area.

Directions: From St. Cloud, go twenty-four miles south on Vermont Avenue/Canoe Creek Road (CR 523) to the Prairie Lakes/Lake Jackson entrance sign on the right (west) side of the road. Use this entrance for the wildlife drive.

Open twenty-four hours a day. Best months for birding are October–April.

352/732-1225.

www.floridaconservation.org.

A Vote for the Land

Ann Morrow

Land speculators beware. Never underestimate the power of the registered voter. Case in point: For about the cost of a pizza per household per year, the citizens of Brevard County have found a way to help protect scrub-jays and gopher tortoises, wet prairies and sand pine scrubs. These folks voted to tax themselves so that the extra funds could be used to purchase native Florida habitats in their home county. Brevard County isn't unique in this respect—twenty-one Florida counties and cities have adopted ballot measures to fund conservation land acquisition. On the land they've purchased—bankrupt properties, ranches, land slated for houses and shopping centers and golf courses, you name it—they've created nature centers, birding spots, refuges for endangered species, and sanctuaries for the human spirit as well.

"Land . . . they ain't makin' it anymore." This oft-repeated quote by the late cowboy-comic Will Rogers says it all. In the past fifty years, almost one-quarter of Florida's forests and wetlands have been cleared to accommodate the human population. We can't get that back. And the hunger for land seems insatiable in this state, where a dizzying growth rate is expected to swell the population to 20 million by 2010.

In response to these pressures, Florida has developed one of the most aggressive land acquisition programs in the United States. In the past twenty-five years, the state has spent $2.8 billion to conserve 2.1 million acres. As a result, 13,000 of Florida's 54,000 square miles have been set aside as public conservation lands. This has been accomplished with the help of land-buying programs such as Save Our Coasts, Save Our Rivers, Conservation and Recreation Lands (CARL), and Florida Preservation 2000. Florida Forever is the successor to Florida Preservation 2000, and it will dedicate $300 million each year through 2010 to buy conservation and recreation lands.

This range of land-buying tools has empowered communities to fight the sprawl and urban growth that has quickly consumed their many cherished landscapes. For example, Brevard County's land-buying program started in 1990, when 60 percent of the voters said yes to the idea of a small property tax surcharge to fund an Environmentally Endangered Lands (EEL) program. Properties such as the Pine Island Conservation Area (site 82) and the Malabar Scrub Sanctuary (site 111) were purchased this way. Their pine flatwoods, marsh, and scrub habitats are home to the Florida scrub-jay, red-tailed hawks, osprey, and a variety of wading birds. Brevard County partnered with the state's CARL Program and the St. Johns River Water Management District in order to expand the funds available to them.

Voters in Seminole and St. Lucie Counties also passed referenda and, like Brevard County, have purchased and preserved cypress swamps, marshes, swamps, pine flatwoods, and other ecological strongholds. Now birdwatchers can visit properties such as the Geneva Wilderness Area (site 57), Lake Jesup Wilderness Area (site 53), and Lake Proctor Wilderness Area (site 56) in Seminole County, and the Indrio Savannahs (site 131) and Pinelands (site 134) in St. Lucie County. They'll be able to watch sandhill cranes and bald eagles and listen to barred owls and yellow-billed cuckoos.

Some community land-buying programs are large and ambitious. Jacksonville, for instance, plans to create permanent green space in 10 percent of its remaining developable property. On a smaller scale, 187 acres of riverfront were added to Tomoka State Park (site 35), thanks to a voter approved referendum in the city of Ormond Beach.

Whatever the size, the result is the same: Vote by vote, acre by acre, cities and counties around Florida are incrementally building up the base of conservation land in Florida. They are finding the results wholly satisfying—and certainly worth the price of a pizza.

Migrant Fallout Cluster

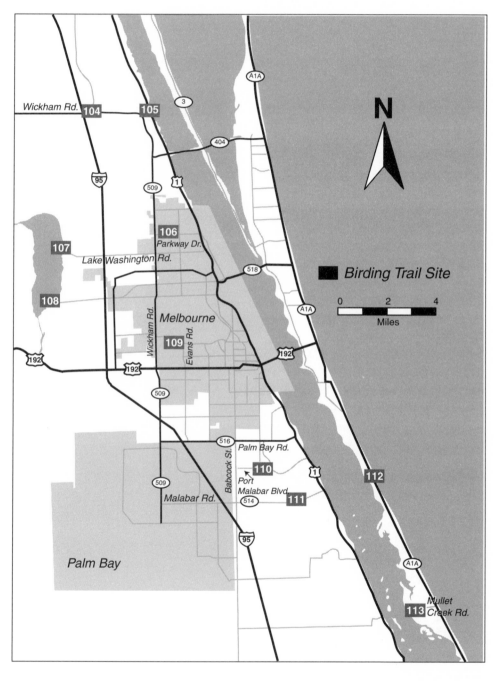

104. Brevard Zoo 144

105. Rotary Park at Suntree 144

106. Wickham Park 145

107. Lake Washington Park 145

108. Lake Washington: Sarno Road Extension 145

109. Erna Nixon Park 146

110. Turkey Creek Sanctuary 146

111. Malabar Scrub Sanctuary 147

112. Coconut Point Park 147

113. Honest John's Fish Camp 148

104. Brevard Zoo

DESCRIPTION: An educational site that's a great option for midday hours when birding is least productive, the Brevard Zoo's native animal area provides up-close looks at species like scarlet ibis and crested caracara, and offers programs on their conservation. A guided kayaking program is available through an on-site wetland and maple slough, where you can see wild wading birds, ducks, and songbirds. Programs for groups of fifteen people or more can be scheduled by calling in advance for details and reservations.

DIRECTIONS: From I-95 north of Melbourne, go east on Wickham Road to the second light. The zoo will be on the right (south) side of the road at the intersection of Wickham and Murrell.

Open 10:00 a.m to 5:00 P.M. Best months for birding are January–December.

(321) 254-9453 x19.

www.brevardzoo.org.

105. Rotary Park at Suntree

DESCRIPTION: Suntree is worth a quick stop in fall and winter. At low tide, waders and shorebirds feed along its shoreline, and at the north end of the property a small sheltered bay harbors wintering ducks like lesser scaup, American wigeon, and pintails, as well as loons and grebes.

DIRECTIONS: From the intersection of SR 404 and US 1, take US 1 north two miles. The park is on the right (east) side of the road.

Open sunrise to sunset. Best months for birding are October–March.

(321) 952-4650.

www.brevardparks.com.

106. Wickham Park

DESCRIPTION: Wickham Park's scrubby flatwoods are home to brown-headed nuthatches and bobwhite, painted buntings and chuck-will's-widows. Birding by ear is helpful in this park, so it may be frustrating for beginners. The open playing fields are good for raptors and killdeer, while the wooded nature trails provide good chances for migrants—thirty or more species of songbirds have been cumulatively recorded for this property. Upon entering the park, pick up a map at the office on the right.

DIRECTIONS: From I-95 north of Melbourne, take Wickham Road east and then south six miles. Turn left (east) onto Parkway Drive. Wickham Park will be half a mile on the left (north) side of the road.

Open sunrise to sunset. Best months for birding are October–April.

(321)952-4650.

www.brevardparks.com.

107 and 108. Lake Washington Park

DESCRIPTION: Lake Washington is one of the first in a chain of lakes that give birth to the St. Johns River. Look for wading birds, bald eagles, purple gallinules, and limpkins on the park's waterfront. Snail kites live on the lake and can be seen occasionally from this vantage. However, they are better viewed at the southeast corner of the lake from the dirt road—Sarno Road Extension (site 108). Sparrows like the fallow edges of the park, and bobolinks can be found in spring and fall migration. Marsh and sedge wrens have been seen at this site. Both Lake Washington accesses are boat launches and can have heavy traffic on weekends; Sarno Road Extension is used primarily to launch airboats, which can be loud and make birding difficult.

DIRECTIONS: From US 1 north of Melbourne, take Lake Washington Road west six miles to the park at the end.

Open sunrise to sunset. Best months for birding are January–December.

(321) 952-4650.

www.brevardparks.com.

109. Erna Nixon Park

DESCRIPTION: This small county park contains upland habitat favored by migratory songbirds and may provide a quick stop to augment your day list. Its educational facilities are by far its strong point, however, with excellent programming and an in-depth native plant walk to teach you more about the habitats upon which Florida's birds depend. Regular guided hikes are held weekends at 2:00 P.M., others by appointment. Bird the property in the morning, watching for summer tanagers, eastern towhees, and mixed warbler flocks in migration.

DIRECTIONS: From I-95 in Melbourne, take US 192 east to Evans Road. Turn left (north) on Evans Road and go 0.8 miles to the park on the left (west) side of the road.

Open 9:00 A.M. to 5:00 P.M. Best months for birding are October–April.

(321) 952-4650.

www.brevardparks.com.

110. Turkey Creek Sanctuary

DESCRIPTION: Turkey Creek is well known throughout the state as a hot spot for warblers and other neotropical migratory songbirds. Its songbird list alone has more than thirty species, including Canada, Nashville, Swainson's, and Tennessee warblers. Migration at this site is most heavily concentrated in October and again in April, and its songbird counts receive statewide recognition during those months. The boardwalk trail winds along Turkey Creek through hardwood hammocks and past a sand pine ridge. The nature center on-site offers regular birding tours in season; call ahead for details and reservations.

DIRECTIONS: From I-95 in Palm Bay, take Palm Bay Road (SR 516) east to Babcock Street and turn right (south). Make a left (east) onto Port Malabar Boulevard and continue east one mile to the Palm Bay Community Center on the right. Parking for the sanctuary is behind the Community Center.

Open 7:00 A.M. to sunset. Best months for birding are March–May, October–November.

(321) 952-3433.

111. Malabar Scrub Sanctuary

DESCRIPTION: Part of Brevard County's Environmentally Endangered Lands program, the Malabar Scrub Sanctuary shelters excellent examples of scrub habitat with breeding populations of scrub-jays. The paved road that bisects the preserve is accessible to the physically challenged, although the sandy scrub trails provide better opportunities for viewing scrub-jays and other birds, including songbird migrants, woodpeckers, sparrows, and eastern towhees. Enter from the south side of the property, checking the map first. Interpretive loop trails occur throughout the site, leaving from the central paved road. Morning hours are best for viewing birds on this site and avoiding the heat and full sun of scrub.

DIRECTIONS: From I-95 in Palm Bay, go east on Malabar Road (SR 514) approximately two and a half miles. The entrance is on the left (north) side of the road immediately east of the fire station.

Open 7:00 A.M. to sunset. Best months for birding are November–May.

(321) 255-4466.

www.eelbrevard.com.

112. Coconut Point Park

DESCRIPTION: A small beach park in the Archie Carr National Wildlife Refuge, Coconut Point warrants a quick stop to check for shorebirds on the beach such as black-bellied plovers and red knots in fall and winter, and to scope for gannets and seabirds offshore. Passing fishing boats frequently draw flocks of seabirds, such as gulls, terns, and jaegers, which may be of interest. Watch the surf for common and red-throated loons in winter.

DIRECTIONS: From Melbourne, take US 192 east to A1A. Go south 5.5 miles; the site is on the left (east) side of the road.

Open sunrise to sunset. Best months for birding are October–April.

(321) 952-4650.

www.brevardparks.com.

113. Honest John's Fish Camp

DESCRIPTION: Honest John's offers a unique access to the Mullet Creek Islands in the Indian River Lagoon. These are the site of wading bird roosts and rookeries, which can be viewed by small motorboat, kayak, or canoe (available for rent on-site). Nesting and resting birds are particularly vulnerable to disturbance; this is an opportunity to view them while learning at the same time about responsible birdwatching, for the benefit of birds and birders alike. A few of the species you're likely to see are great egrets, anhingas, snowy egrets, tricolored herons, great blue herons, roseate spoonbills, black- and yellow-crowned night herons, and white ibis.

DIRECTIONS: From Melbourne Beach, take SR A1A ten miles south to Mullet Creek Road. Turn right (west); Honest John's is at the end of the road. Please respect the private property along this road by not leaving your car until you've reached the fish camp.

Open 6:00 A.M. to 6:00 P.M., closed Christmas Day, and Tuesdays from May through October. Best months for birding are October–April.

(321) 727-2923.

www.honestjohns.net.

Made in the Shade

Ann Morrow

Coffee drinking and birdwatching—what possible link could there be between these two pleasures? Think tree canopies and migrating songbirds, and two major pieces of an emerging conservation issue converge.

It comes down to birds and what they eat. Whether they are connoisseurs of insects, nectar, fruit, or seeds, most birds opt to spend time in forests that offer the greatest variety of food for the least effort. The most food-rich forests are usually the most complex. That is, they feature diverse species of trees and shrubs growing at different heights.

In traditional or shade coffee plantations, the shrubby coffee plants are cultivated beneath the canopy of a natural forest or a forest planted with, in some cases, up to forty different species of trees that add nitrogen to the soil and provide wood or fruit to the grower. Studies have shown that these traditionally managed coffee plantations support more than 150 bird species—only an undisturbed tropical forest supports more birds. The forest aids in the production of coffee by anchoring and nourishing the soil. Insect pests such as the coffee berry borer are kept under control by the forest's insectivorous birds, both resident and migratory. For obvious reasons, coffee grown on these traditional plantations is referred to as "shade-grown" or "bird-friendly" or "songbird" coffee.

Threatening this successful blend of sound agricultural practices and biodiversity is "sun coffee," the sun-loving hybrid coffee varieties that have come into production in the last twenty years. Sun coffee produces higher yields, but at the expense of forested habitats. Sun coffee plantations also offer little food variety and attract few birds. According to the Smithsonian Migratory Bird Center, studies in Colombia and Mexico found 94 to 97 percent fewer bird species in sun-grown coffee plantations than in shade-grown coffee plantations. This makes sense when you consider that within shade coffee plantations, more than two-thirds of the birds are found in the canopy; fewer than 10 percent forage in the coffee plants.

Besides clearing forests, the production of sun coffee usually requires an infusion of chemical fertilizers, pesticides, and herbicides that are not needed in shade plantations where the tree canopy protects the soil, shades out the weeds, and attracts birds that manage pests. As undisturbed forest habitat disappears in coffee-growing nations, traditional coffee plantations serve as important sanctuaries for resident birds, such as parrots and toucans, and for the more than two hundred species of neotropical migratory birds. A neotropical migrant is a bird that breeds in North America and winters in Mexico, Central or South America, or the Caribbean Islands. The majority of these are songbirds, such as the wood thrush, painted bunting, and scarlet tanager, but some shorebirds, raptors, and waterfowl are also considered neotropical.

The United States consumes about one-third of the world's coffee supply. As consumers, we can cast votes with our dollars, by purchasing shade-grown coffee that supports traditional coffee plantations and the birds and other wildlife dependent on their forest canopies. Coffee labeled as shade-grown or bird-friendly has been promoted for several years by conservation organizations such as the American Birding Association, the Smithsonian Migratory Bird Center, and the Rainforest Alliance. Some of these organizations and a growing number of vendors offer shade-grown coffee through mail order or specialty shops.

Admirers of orioles, hummingbirds, warblers, and hundreds of other migratory birds look forward to the day when they can walk into any coffee shop and order "One bird-friendly cappuccino to go, please!" In the meantime, we can drink such coffee at home.

It's a Matter of Survival

Shorebirds on the Beach

Nancy Douglass

I'm a worrier. I come by it honestly. My parents taught me well. They worried about their children's health and my father's job. But not me—I worry about the birds.

This morning, I am worried about red knots. I am sitting on the beach with my binoculars trained on a flock of the weary migrants. As I watch, a little boy runs toward the birds, scattering them in all directions. After momentary chaos, they reconvene in midair, wheel, bank back toward me in fluid acrobatic flight, and once again settle down to earth. It's about the fifth time I have witnessed this maneuver in as many minutes, and I'm worried. I'm concerned that these hemispheric globetrotters may not survive their journey across the Gulf to their wintering grounds in South America. The few hours surrounding peak high tide are their only opportunity to rest their fatigued flight muscles. When the tide falls, briefly exposing mudflats surrounding this barrier island, they must begin the serious task of feeding, gathering every calorie they can. Just fifty years ago these birds had the shore largely to themselves. Now their metabolic equation must deal with the cost of being flushed from their feeding and roosting grounds as often as every few minutes. In human terms, this is like requiring a marathon runner to stop every ten yards of her race to perform three pushups.

Although the dropping tide is barely discernable to me, the birds have responded. First, the tallest and longest-legged—a great blue heron and two reddish egrets—move out onto the flats. Next, a few snowy egrets and some willets follow their lead. Finally, as the water fully recedes, hundreds of short-legged shorebirds, including red knots, burst past me onto the mudflats. They settle in choreographed groups to feed on the emerging landscape.

In the distance I hear an engine drone and spot a "flats boat" hurtling down the backside of the island. The birds respond by blowing off their feeding grounds as the boat races by. Several minutes later, they settle back down to feed. Now two jet-skis zigzag along the edge of the flats, occasionally charging a large aggregation of birds just to see them fly. Another boat pulls up to one of the sandbars and begins unloading picnicking supplies. A large black dog leaps off the stern and chases the remaining birds off the flats. The beachgoers and boaters are completely unaware of their role in the birds' struggle for survival—but, watching the harried birds, I'm worried.

As I trek back up the beach, I come to a large, open sandy area where people lounge in the sun. A young couple throws a frisbee. What the beachgoers don't know is that in spring, this is where beach-nesting shorebirds—least terns, maybe black skimmers or snowy plovers—will come to nest. I will worry about them too. They will lay their camouflaged eggs directly on the ground, in shallow nest scrapes. With every passerby they will fly off their nests and attempt to defend their patch of sand by noisily dive-bombing the intruders. Meanwhile, the eggs and chicks will be at the mercy of the searing summer heat, hungry crows and gulls, and the heavy feet of unsuspecting pedestrians.

Along with my coworkers all over the state, I will post signs around the perimeter of the nesting area. I know that most people will honor these temporary signs, but it will take only one thoughtless person or one unleashed dog to undo an entire season's worth of nesting effort. Still, it is good to do more than just worry.

Vero Vireo Cluster

114. T. M. Goodwin Waterfowl Management Area   154

115. St. Sebastian River State Buffer Preserve (North Entrance)   154

116. St. Sebastian River State Buffer Preserve (South Entrance)   154

117. Sebastian Inlet State Park   155

118. Environmental Learning Center   156

119. Blue Cypress Conservation Area   157

120. Indian River County Wetlands Treatment Facility   157

121. Oslo Riverfront Conservation Area (ORCA)   158

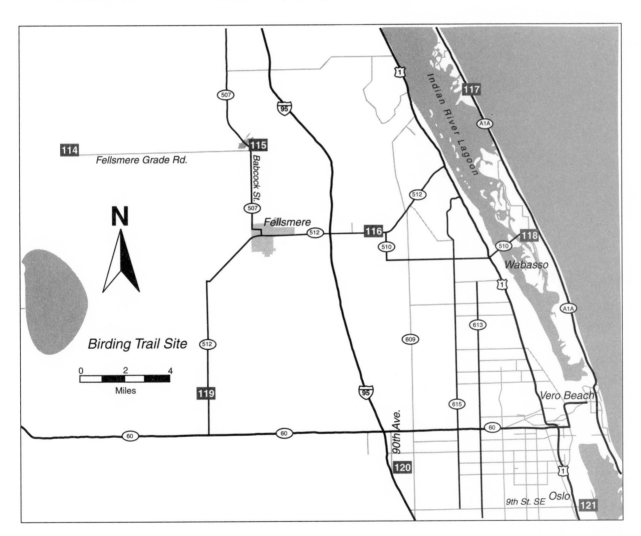

114. T. M. Goodwin Waterfowl Management Area

DESCRIPTION: One of the premier duck hunting areas in the state, T. M. Goodwin can make for some pretty interesting birding too! Expect to find the gamut of ducks from late fall through winter, as well as shorebirds and hawks in migration. The area is closed to birders when hunts are going on, so call in advance for access information. View the birds by hiking the series of dikes around the impoundments. The road into the area can also be good for everything from swallow-tailed kites to bobwhite to crested caracara.

DIRECTIONS: From the intersection of I-95 and CR 512 north of Vero Beach, go west three miles to Babcock Street (CR 507). Turn right (north) and go five miles. Turn left (west) onto Fellsmere Grade Road just south of the C-54 canal. Follow it to the Stick Marsh boat ramp and follow the signs to the entrance to the waterfowl management area.

Open one hour before sunrise to one hour after sunset. Best months for birding are October–April.

(321) 726-2862.

http://wld.fwc.state.fl.us/duck.

115 and 116. St. Sebastian River State Buffer Preserve

DESCRIPTION: The wild St. Sebastian River preserve offers excellent views of sought-after species like scrub-jays, Bachman's sparrows, red-cockaded woodpeckers, and raptors. Start at the visitor center at the north entrance on Buffer Preserve Drive. Pick up a map and a bird list, and perhaps check the brief interpretive trail. Bachman's sparrows, scrub-jays, and red-cockaded woodpeckers can all be found on the northeast portion of the horse trail accessed via Stumper Flats Trail on the east side of the property. On the west side, near the intersection of Buffer Preserve Drive and CR 507, the Green, Blue, and Red Trails wind through hydric hammock excellent for migratory songbirds and swallow-tailed kites. The south entrance to the property, off CR 512 east of I-95, has more open space, with good views of raptors and meadowlarks. Plan for rustic conditions, good hiking, and a rewarding birding experience.

Directions: From I-95 north of Vero Beach, exit at CR 512. For the north entrance of the preserve, head west three miles to Babcock Street (CR 507). Turn right and go five miles. Immediately after crossing the C-54 canal, Buffer Preserve Drive will be on the right (east) side of the road; take this to the visitor center. For the south entrance of the preserve, head east from exit 69 of I-95 for 1.8 miles to W. W. Ranch Road. Turn left (north) and follow the road into the preserve.

Open 8:00 A.M. to 5:00 P.M. Best months for birding are October–April.

(321) 953-5004.

www.dep.state.fl.us/coastal/sites.

117. Sebastian Inlet State Park

Description: The state park spans both sides of the Sebastian Inlet and both sides of the barrier island on which it is located. With beach and river frontage, it has a diversity of wading birds and shorebirds, views of the ocean for offshore species like gannets, jaegers, and petrels, and mangrove margins popular for migratory songbirds. When you arrive, pick up a bird list and map at the entrance stations on the northwest side of the inlet bridge. Upon driving in, you will notice a small cove on the northwest side of the bridge, which is good for waders and shorebirds. The western foot trails along the small spit of land into the river offer a good vantage to scope for ducks, loons, and grebes in the river during fall and winter. Check the ocean side for shorebirds like turnstones and plovers, and watch for terns and gulls. On the southwest side of the bridge, the entrance to the fishing museum takes you past a dock where wood storks congregate and on through the campground to a spit of land good for shorebirds. An entrance 0.4 miles south of the fishing museum entrance offers a trail through diked mangrove impoundments which are good for migratory songbirds in early October and making landfall again in April. The park also contracts with a concessionaire to provide guided boat tours to

Pelican Island National Wildlife Refuge, a fabulous site to see nesting and roosting waders. Call ahead for reservations.

DIRECTIONS: Take A1A north twelve miles from Vero Beach. The entrance station for the site is on the north side of the Sebastian Inlet bridge, on the left (west) side of the road.

Open twenty-four hours a day. Best months for birding are January–December.

(321) 984-4852.

www.dep.state.fl.us/parks.

118. Environmental Learning Center

DESCRIPTION: This nature center fronts on the Indian River Lagoon, providing an easy access for educational adventures with all the lagoon's wildlife, birds included. Wading birds galore, including roseate spoonbills and reddish egrets, use the lagoon for food and shelter—come learn how, and see them in action! The center itself is free, so peruse their displays and bird their boardwalk through the mangroves. Hands-on field trips, from kayaking by moonlight to Family Birding 101, are reasonably priced, so call ahead for schedules and details. Great for a family afternoon, or those times when the birds are smart enough to stay out of the sun, and so should you!

DIRECTIONS: From Vero Beach, take US 1 north to Wabasso. Turn right (east) on CR 510. Cross the causeway over the Indian River Lagoon. Turn right on Wabasso Island Lane before the tall bridge. The ELC is ahead on the right.

Open Tuesday through Friday, 10:00 A.M. to 4:00 P.M.; Saturday, 9:00 A.M. to 12:00 P.M. (to 4:00 P.M. in winter); Sunday, 1:00 to 4:00 P.M. Best months for birding are January–December.

(772) 589-5050.

www.elcweb.org.

119. Blue Cypress Conservation Area

DESCRIPTION: Blue Cypress features a series of impounded marshes harboring migratory and resident ducks as well as a diversity of wading birds including limpkins. Purple gallinules have been seen on the site, as have both bitterns, king rails, sora, fulvous whistling ducks, snail kites, and crested caracaras. From the parking area, you may walk in several directions—check the kiosk map to choose which is right for you. One of the westbound dikes will offer more remote, sometimes higher-quality birding. However, these paths are narrower with irregular surfaces. A north-south dike offers a wider, smoother walking surface, although the path is more exposed and birds are harder to spot. This site is best in fall, winter, and spring. Summer is hot on the exposed dikes, and the mosquitoes can be challenging. There is seasonal hunting in the vicinity but not on the levees. Also, there is some airboating in the canals, so be careful if you choose to canoe.

DIRECTIONS: From Vero Beach, take SR 60 west. Seven and one-half miles past I-95, turn right (north) on CR 512. Drive a mile and a half and turn left (west) into the parking area.

Open twenty-four hours a day. Best months for birding are October–April.

http://sjr.state.fl.us.

120. Indian River County Wetlands Treatment Facility

DESCRIPTION: This water treatment facility uses an innovative technique developed in the late 1980s to polish its treated wastewater. After chemical cleaning, the water, which in the recent past would have been immediately discharged into a river, flows instead through a created wetland. This wetland uses plants like cattail and bulrush to remove excess nutrients like phosphates and nitrates, so that when the water is finally discharged into a creek, it won't cause an algae bloom that chokes out the native aquatic life. Needless to say, these wetlands are very productive, and wading birds love them for foraging! This site is distinguished by its boardwalk and overlook system through the diked impoundments, allowing easy viewing of the wading birds (including egrets, herons, glossy and white ibises, both bitterns), ducks (wood, green-winged and blue-winged teal, mottled, northern shoveler, gadwall, American wigeon, and ring-necked), and associated water- and shorebirds (moorhens, purple gallinules, king rails, sora, snipe, stilts, and both yellowlegs, among others). Please check in at the office before birding.

Directions: From I-95 exit at Vero Beach on SR 60. Go east one light to 90th Avenue and turn right (south). Proceed to 8th Street and turn left (east). The wetlands facility will be approximately three-quarters of a mile on the right (south).

Open Monday through Friday, 7:00 A.M. to 3:30 P.M.; weekends 7:00 A.M. to 3:30 P.M. by appointment. Best months for birding are October–April.

(561) 770-5045.

121. Oslo Riverfront Conservation Area (ORCA)

Description: ORCA is a unique citizen-government cooperative effort. Purchased by the county as an environmentally important property, it has a committed friends group who worked first for its acquisition and now work for its augmentation with educational signage, boardwalks, trails, and overlooks. The Herb Kale Trail—named for one of Florida's preeminent ornithologists of all time—begins through hardwood hammock good for songbird migrants, and continues into the mangrove swamps and impoundment areas. In these impoundments, from the trail or the overlook, you can easily see wading birds, shorebirds, and ducks. Canoes can be rented from the adjacent University of Florida Medical Entomology Lab, compliments of the Pelican Island Audubon Society. By canoe, you can paddle beyond the mangrove forest to see shorebirds and wading birds feeding, loafing, and nesting on spoil islands and bars in the Indian River Lagoon. As always, use optics to view these birds so that you can keep your distance and ensure their well-being. Free birding tours run on Saturday mornings; call ahead for details, or to make arrangements for a personalized tour for your birding group.

Directions: Take US 1 south from Vero Beach to Oslo Road (9th Street SE). Turn left (east); the site will be about half a mile on the left (north) side of the road.

Open sunrise to sunset. Best months for birding are October–April.

(561) 778-7200.

Crested Caracara

Florida Prairie Specialty

Joan Morrison

The world of the crested caracara is wide and flat. Overhead a summer sky blazes, pulling steam from the earth minutes after a drenching rain. In the green crown of a cabbage palm, an adolescent caracara shakes the water from her back and begins a languid preen in the late morning sun. Beneath her perch a vast pasture spreads to the horizon, dotted with stands of palm and small hammocks of scrubby oak.

In all of Florida, the crested caracara is unique. It is the only member of this distinctive group of raptors found in the Southeast; outside the state, the nearest populations are in Cuba and Texas. The bird's current breeding range in Florida includes at least eight counties in the south-central region of the peninsula, with strongholds in Highlands, Glades, Okeechobee, DeSoto, and Osceola Counties (see the Scrub and Stream Cluster, the aptly named Caracara Cluster, and the Whooping Crane Cluster in this book). Here it is a bird largely reliant on private tracts of upland cattle pasture, a sizeable but shrinking block of real estate as attractive to developers as to caracaras.

In the field, the crested caracara is unmistakable. Though in fact a falcon, it has a decidedly hawklike build and bearing. Most often it will be perched conspicuously on a fence post or telephone pole, with its long yellow legs and tail distinguishing it from crows or vultures, even in silhouette. Closer inspection leads to greater certainty: the crested caracara sports a regal cap of black feathers, a long yellow-orange face, and a bluish bill. Its body is mostly black, but the feathers of the neck and breast and upper back are white-tipped with horizontal black bars.

While often seen scavenging road-killed animals, the caracara is actually a diet generalist, feeding on small mammals, birds, snakes, frogs, fish, and insects as well as carrion and scraps. Unlike most raptors, caracaras rarely swoop down on prey from above; rather, look for them walking about on the ground, sometimes in groups, foraging in pastures or along wetland edges. They are opportunists and can be seen in newly plowed fields, along recently cleaned ditches, and in freshly burned pastures feeding on prey exposed by these activities.

Caracaras are most regularly observed from January to March as they forage to feed their growing young. Unlike other falcons, caracaras do build nests, bulky structures of twigs and vines placed almost exclusively in cabbage palms. Both adults share parental duties, and the young remain with their parents for several months after fledging. Juvenile plumage resembles the adult in pattern, but is brownish overall with a buffy neck and vertical brown streaks instead of horizontal bars on the breast feathers.

The crested caracara is now threatened in Florida, primarily because of loss of grassland and pasture habitat to agricultural and urban development. The number of breeding pairs is directly related to the amount of suitable nesting habitat, and recent studies indicate that most suitable habitat is already occupied. Also of concern are collisions with vehicles, which account for more than half the mortality of young caracaras. And as large conspicuous raptors, caracaras are still sometimes shot, poisoned, or trapped.

The future of Florida's crested caracaras is complex and uncertain, and it will involve people, land use, and economic issues. The fact that most pairs live on privately owned cattle ranches necessitates the cooperation of ranchers, scientists, and land management agencies in conservation planning. As always, education is of prime importance. The better we know and understand this striking species, the more incentive there will be to work toward ensuring its continued survival in Florida.

Scrub and Stream Cluster

122. Highlands Hammock State Park   162

123. Istokpoga Park   162

124. Hickory Hammock   163

125. Lake June-in-Winter Scrub State Park   164

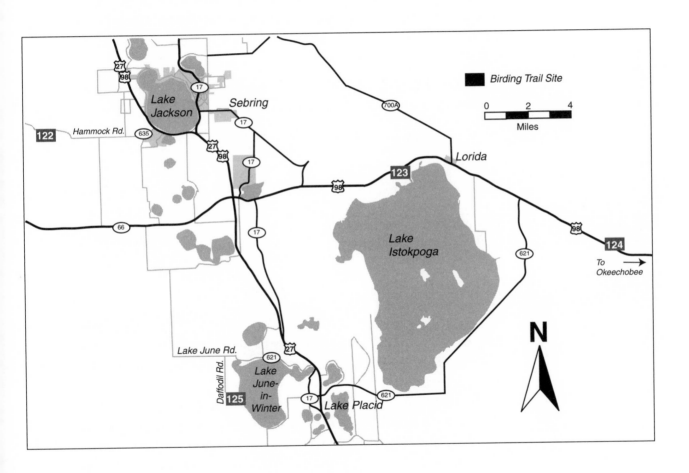

122. Highlands Hammock State Park

DESCRIPTION: The aptly named Highlands Hammock State Park includes a combination of scrubby uplands and towering hammocks where swallow-tailed kites often nest in spring and early summer. At the entrance gate, pick up a park map and ask about scheduled educational programming. For scrub and flatwoods species, veer right, pass through the campground, and hike the biking trails. Neotropical migrants and wading bird species can be seen by following the road straight into the park and driving the hammock loop. At the midpoint of the loop, the cypress swamp trail takes a catwalk through a wetland where you can see a diversity of wading bird species, including wood storks. As with much hammock birding, birds are often in the canopy, so this is a good opportunity to practice your birding by ear. Guided tram tours are available, as are educational programs and tours, if you call ahead for reservations. Bikes may be rented on-site.

DIRECTIONS: From US 27 on the north side of Sebring, take Hammock Road (CR 635) three miles west to the park entrance.

Open 8:00 A.M. to sunset. Best months for birding are September–May.

(863) 386-6094.

www.dep.state.fl.us/parks.

123. Istokpoga Park

DESCRIPTION: A small county park sits on the north shore of vast Lake Istokpoga. This lake has one of the largest numbers of osprey nests in the country, as well as wading bird colonies of considerable biological importance on islands at its center. When approaching the park from the southeast on SR 98, watch the pastures on the south side of the road for caracara. The park itself has a boat launch and dock out into the lake. Scan the boat basin for wading birds, including limpkins, and scope the lake for wintering ducks. Ring-necked ducks are very common here in winter. Then follow the trail along the water's edge to the east and then north along the boardwalk through the cypress margin. This margin is frequented by migrant and breeding songbirds alike. Highlands County hopes to acquire adjacent property and extend the trail system all the way to Arbuckle Creek; watch in coming years for this addition, as it would promise excellent birdwatching opportunities.

DIRECTIONS: From the intersection of US 27 and SR 98, four miles south of Sebring, take SR 98 northeast eight miles. Istokpoga Park is on the right (south) side of the road, just on the east side of the Arbuckle Creek bridge, in the town of Lorida.

Open sunrise to sunset. Best months for birding are October–April.

(863) 386-6812.

124. Hickory Hammock

DESCRIPTION: Hickory Hammock is worth a stop if you have the time and are driving SR 98 between Okeechobee and Sebring. On the north side of SR 98 immediately on the west side of the Kissimmee River, there is an entrance good for a quick owl prowl. Barred, barn, screech, and great horned owls inhabit the thick hammock and abandoned schoolhouse area at the entrance. If you don't find the birds, check beneath the big oak in front of the house for owl pellets. There is another entrance to the property approximately three miles northwest on SR 98. Watch for scrub-jays on telephone wires, and burrowing owls and caracaras in pastures all along US 98. The entrance to Hickory Hammock is on the north side of the road, and marks the trailhead to several miles of trail through xeric oak hammock and scrub habitats. Diversity of species is not high, but turkeys and raptors are likely. There is hunting on this property, so check the entrance kiosks for hunt dates.

DIRECTIONS: Hickory Hammock is located between Sebring and Okeechobee on SR 98, just west of the Kissimmee River.

Open sunrise to sunset. Best months for birding are October–April.

(941)462-5260.

125. Lake June-in-Winter Scrub State Park

DESCRIPTION: The Lake June scrub sanctuary is nestled in the highlands of the Lake Wales Ridge, a series of ancient sand dunes that is now home to a number of rare plants and animals found nowhere else in the world. One scrub specialty is the Florida scrub-jay, a resident of this property and a much sought-after species by birders in Florida. For jays, hike the Bobcat Trail south from the entrance gate into the scrub areas of the property. Please stay on the trails to protect fragile plants of the scrub habitat. From the parking area, the brief Tomoka Trail runs through a streamside hammock perfect for neotropical migrants; also, check the lakefront for waders and ducks. Osprey and bald eagles both breed on-site, and pileated, red-bellied, and red-headed woodpeckers are common. Remember scrub is a hot, sandy environment; bring water and a hat. Beekeepers also keep their hives in adjacent orange groves, although they are no cause for concern.

DIRECTIONS: Take US 27 north of Lake Placid to Lake June Road (CR 621). Turn west and go four miles to Daffodil Road. Turn left (south); the park is two miles ahead at the end of Daffodil Road.

Open 8:00 A.M. to sunset. Best months for birding are October–April.

(863) 386-6094.

www.dep.state.fl.us/parks.

Ode to a Sparrow

Paul Gray

In Florida, grasshopper sparrows make their homes in the dry prairie, a subtle, easily overlooked ecosystem in the center of the state. If you explore this habitat up close, you'll see grass, palmettos, and small wetlands. It is tempting to try to discern the horizon, where you can see hazy, gray tree islands, but they are always too distant for a satisfying look—and that's not where the sparrows will be.

Strangely, I think the best way to get to know this vast landscape is to look down by your feet. You'll encounter an amazing structure and variety of plants emerging, and it's here that the sparrows live, mostly on the ground, running among what to them must seem tall forests. They are very shy birds and hard to see. If you approach them on foot, they fly a short distance and drop down in the grass. By the time you have caught up with them again, you find they have run somewhere else.

I have given up trying to observe Florida grasshopper sparrows closely, and now am just content to watch their weak, weaving flights. Seeing one is a gift.

This bird sings only near sunrise and sunset, and its quiet song sounds like the grasshopper for which it is named. But it has another song that shocked me the first time I heard it, soft and surprisingly musical, tinkling up and down persistently, as if it were talking to itself.

The Florida grasshopper sparrow, a subspecies of the far-ranging grasshopper sparrow, is the only grasshopper sparrow breeding within hundreds of miles. The native prairie it depends on has been reduced in Florida by 90 percent during the past thirty-five years, and the sparrow's fortune has followed in kind. We believe only about six hundred Florida grasshopper sparrows remain in the state, ranking them among the most endangered animals in the world.

Virtually all known populations of Florida grasshopper sparrows now occur on conservation lands, including Three Lakes Wildlife Management Area (site 103), Avon Park Air Force Range, Kissimmee Prairie Preserve State Park (site 128), and Audubon's Ordway-Whittell Kissimmee Prairie Sanctuary. Though these endangered birds are protected on these lands, challenges to their survival persist.

For example, dams on private adjoining properties periodically have flooded sparrow habitat at Three Lakes and on Audubon's Ordway-Whittell Sanctuary. Flooding destroys nests and covers food sources, and grasshopper sparrows do not seem to move away when confronted with problems like flooding—they just "stick it out." At Three Lakes, happily, biologists were able to successfully restore the sparrow habitat. On Audubon's Ordway-Whittell Sanctuary, we were not as fortunate. Flooding caused the sparrow's population to drop from about thirty pairs of sparrows on the sanctuary in 1995, to about twenty pairs in 1996, to fourteen pairs in 1997, to perhaps three pairs in 1998, to no birds at all in 1999.

Audubon tried to work with neighboring landowners and state and federal agencies to remedy the flooding problem. After several years and tens of thousands of dollars spent on studies and negotiations, no solutions were found, and Audubon had to file suit in federal court. Audubon won the suit, but by the time the flooding problem was corrected, the sparrows were gone. Long, careful studies and bureaucratic processes do not fit a sparrow's schedule.

Recently, several large tracts of dry prairie have been conserved by the state, most notably the Kissimmee Prairie Preserve State Park, Fisheating Creek, and the Bright Hour Ranch. Hopefully, such acquisitions can preserve not only this special little bird but some of Florida's unique dry prairie ecosystem as well.

Caracara Cluster

126. Prairie Bird Long Loop (Starting Point)   168

127. Prairie Bird Short Loop (Starting Point)   168

128. Kissimmee Prairie Preserve State Park   168

129. Lock 7: Jaycee Park   169

130. Okee-Tantie   170

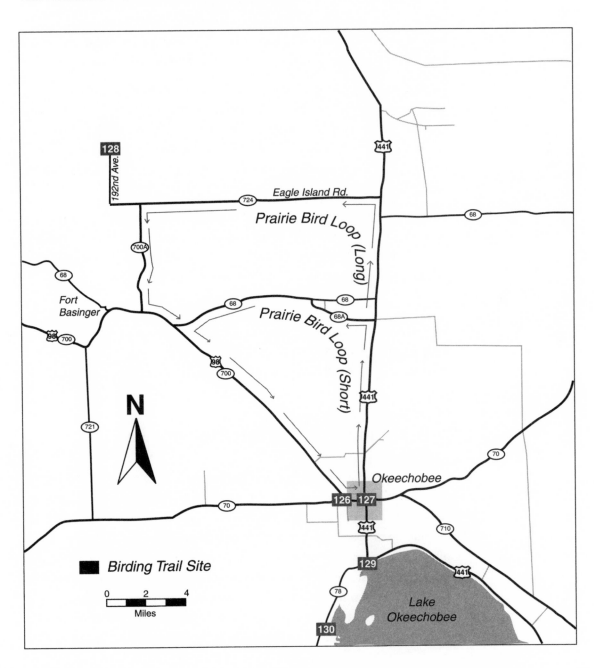

126 and 127. Prairie Bird Loops

DESCRIPTION: Two driving loops based out of the city of Okeechobee give a good overview of the county and of species that may be seen while traveling in the area. On your drive through the cattle country of Okeechobee County, keep your eyes peeled for crested caracaras on fence posts, waders and migratory shorebirds at the muddy margins of watering holes, mottled ducks in the ponds, burrowing owls and sandhill cranes in the pastures, and swallow-tailed kites around the hammocks. Remember to respect private land, and if you stop on the road edge, take care to stay well out of the way of passing traffic.

DIRECTIONS: Long loop (take this loop if you'd like to visit Kissimmee Prairie): From Okeechobee, drive fifteen miles north on US 441 to Eagle Island Road (CR 724). Turn left (west) and go twelve miles to Durrance Road (CR 700A) and turn left (south). Go six miles on CR 700A to US 98 and turn left (southeast). This road will return you to SR 70 just west of Okeechobee, fifteen miles ahead.

Short loop: Again, take US 441 north from Okeechobee, but turn left (west) after nine miles, onto Potter Road (CR 68A). This will become CR 68 and, after ten miles, will intersect US 98. Turn left (southeast) on US 98 and follow it fourteen miles to SR 70, just west of the city of Okeechobee.

Open twenty-four hours a day, year-round. Best months for birding are January–December.

128. Kissimmee Prairie Preserve State Park

DESCRIPTION: Kissimmee Prairie Preserve State Park is one of the last remaining examples of dry prairie in the state of Florida, home to such specialties as the crested caracara and the Florida grasshopper sparrow. A landscape of wide-open space, this property is heartbreakingly beautiful and remote, offering a remarkable birding experience. As you approach, look in the pastures on the west side of the road just before the park entrance to see burrowing owls. Do NOT ENTER THIS PROPERTY—it is privately owned. YOU MAY VIEW THESE OWLS ONLY FROM THE ROAD. Upon entering the park, visit the entrance kiosk for a map and information. By hiking Peavine Trail past Military Grade, you will come to a slough full of alligators and wading birds. Hiking Military Grade to the west instead will take you past prime Florida grasshopper sparrow habitat, although they're likely to be seen only in the spring when males are singing to advertise their territory and their availability to a mate. The Grade runs several miles through oak hammock and past prairie, eventually ending at the Kissimmee River edge where short-tailed hawks have been seen. Raptors and turkeys, wood storks and warblers are seen throughout the trip. Military Grade is more than ten miles one-way, so a bike is helpful to make the entire trip. This area is wild, so be sure to pick up a map and bring water and a hat. For the birder willing to invest the time and energy, Kissimmee Prairie is an experience you won't soon forget.

DIRECTIONS: From Okeechobee, go north on US 441 to Eagle Island Road (CR 724). Turn left (west) and go eight miles to the stop sign. Continue for another one mile to 192nd Avenue (Peavine Road). Turn right (north) and go five miles to the park entrance.

Open 8:00 A.M. to sunset. Best months for birding are October–April.

(863) 462-5360.

www.dep.state.fl.us/parks.

129. Lock 7: Jaycee Park

DESCRIPTION: The Lock 7 park beside Lake Okeechobee has the usual assemblage of Florida wading birds, including herons, egrets, and ibis, but it also has a particular allure for terns, skimmers, and gulls: flocks of thousands of skimmers sometimes loaf in the parking lot in fall and winter. Royal, Caspian, and least terns sometimes join them, and the area has been known to have its share of rare gull sightings. If birds are loafing, approach them in your car rather than on foot, to minimize disturbance. Watch for brown pelicans, white pelicans, cormorants, anhingas, loons, and grebes offshore as well.

DIRECTIONS: From Okeechobee, take US 441 south three miles to SR 78. Turn right (west) and take an immediate left to cross over the Hoover Dike. Jaycee Park is immediately on the lake side of the dike.

Open sunrise to sunset. Best months for birding are January–December.

1-800-871-4403.

130. Okee-Tantie

Description: If you're already down by the lake, a stop is in order at Okee-Tantie, with its fishing boats and wood stork regulars. Look for waders in the boat basins, woodpeckers and songbirds in the edges. From the easternmost point you can scope the lake for ducks and look at a blue heron rookery.

Directions: The site is five miles west of the intersection of SR 78 and US 441. Okee-Tantie is on the south side of the road at the Kissimmee River bridge.

Open twenty-four hours a day. Best months for birding are January–December.

1-800-871-4403.

Un-straightening the Kissimmee River

Paul Gray

Because my home is on one side of the Kissimmee River and my office on the other, I get to drive along the river and cross its floodplain twice each workday. The green pastures, orange groves, patches of scrub, caracaras sitting on posts, the remnant river run, and even the C-38 canal all make the drive quietly interesting. About halfway along the drive, on the bluff overlooking the floodplain, rests an ancient Indian mound, perhaps thirty feet tall, with old oaks bristling outward. The mound makes my thoughts cross time: What did these ancient people see when they looked out over this landscape? Would they recognize this place now, or have we erased those things that made up the real Florida?

What has clearly been lost since the time of those ancient people is the Kissimmee River itself, which once meandered for a hundred miles through a two-mile-wide floodplain. Between 1962 and 1971 the river was transformed into a canal, fifty-two miles long, a hundred yards wide, and straight as an arrow. This process consumed one-third of the original river channel and seven thousand acres of adjacent wetlands. Populations of ducks, coots, and wading birds plummeted. In the surrounding uplands, native prairies full of wiregrass, saw palmetto, and an abundance of wildflowers gave way to improved pasture, citrus, or homes. With these areas of storage and replenishment now gone, rainfall reaches the river in the same month it falls and is long gone by the dry season.

The water remaining in the canal and the old river runs has changed too. Today, dissolved oxygen levels frequently drop to levels lethal to fish. The marshes no longer clean the nutrients from surrounding agricultural lands but instead allow direct discharge into Lake Okeechobee.

Congress approved the channelization of the Kissimmee River in 1954, after extreme flooding from the hurricane of 1947 prompted a strong push for flood protection. By 1976, voices for restoration had articulated a clear enough case for the Florida Legislature to pass the Kissimmee River Restoration Act. The legislation called for reengineering of not only the river but also the lakes above it in an effort to help Lake Okeechobee.

Will the restoration work?

In the current plan, about twenty-two miles of the C-38 canal will be filled, thus restoring approximately forty-three miles of river channel and 27,000 acres of wetlands. The plans require the purchase of about 56,000 acres in the lower basin (along the river) and about 28,000 acres above the river to increase the storage capacity of those lakes. Construction commenced in 1999 and should take about ten years to complete. Several miles of the huge old canal have been filled, and already wildlife is using the restored floodplain.

The Kissimmee River may never be the same, but it will be improved significantly. The river will not only function better within the floodplain, it will benefit from other conservation efforts in the watershed. The state bought a 50,000–acre parcel of land to the east of the Kissimmee River—the Kissimmee Prairie Preserve State Park (site 128)—home to the largest contiguous native prairie left in the state. This tract, the adjacent 7,300-acre Audubon Kissimmee Prairie Sanctuary, and the 106,000-acre Avon Park Air Force Range on the west side of the river make an ecosystem-level preserve around the restored river.

Today, the ancient Indians who built the mound would observe many new sights, but they would also recognize large areas of the Florida they knew. It is not all lost, and now, through the continuing efforts of so many, the real Florida can return.

Sandhill Crane Cluster

131. Indrio Savannahs   174

132. Fort Pierce Inlet State Park   174

133. Bear Point Sanctuary   175

134. Pinelands   175

135. Savannas Preserve State Park   176

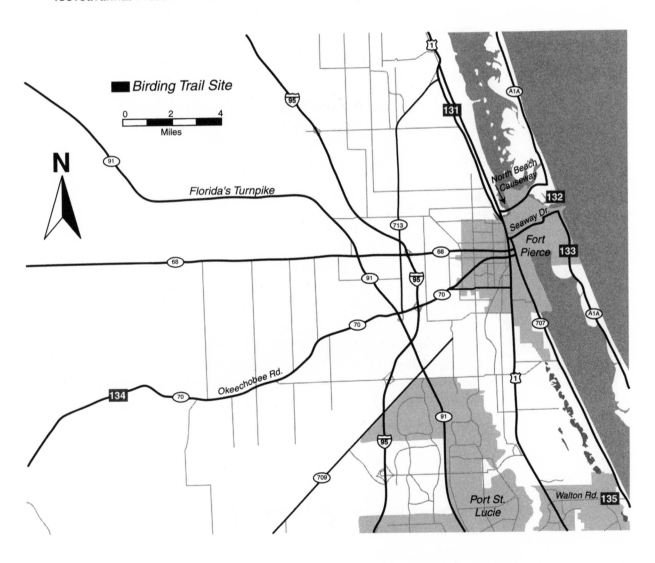

131. Indrio Savannahs

DESCRIPTION: Indrio Savannahs is part of St. Lucie County's environmental lands program, and offers several options for hiking and birding. Upon parking, bird the borrow pit lake margins for snipe, wading birds, and migratory ducks. From there, walk from the south end of the lake across the footbridge onto the dike trail. This trail leads through some wetlands where bitterns, migratory ducks, and waders like wood storks can be found. After returning to the parking area, explore the trail system through the uplands on the west side of the borrow pit lake. Watch for neotropical migrants in the trees, swallow-tailed kites overhead in spring and summer, and Florida scrub-jays in scrub areas.

DIRECTIONS: From Fort Pierce, take US 1 north four miles to Tozour Road. Turn left (west) on Tozour Road. The entrance is at the north end of the road.

Open sunrise to sunset. Best months for birding are October–April.

(772) 462-2525.

www.stlucieco.gov.

132. Fort Pierce Inlet State Park

DESCRIPTION: This site offers a quick opportunity to check for shorebirds, waders, terns, and the like in the Fort Pierce area. After entering the park, drive to the end of the road and bird the southwestern tip of the peninsula, looking for loafing dunlins, dowitchers, terns, skimmers, and others on sand spits on the west side of the point. From the beach side, watch for plovers and willets working the tidal area, and terns and gulls loafing higher up on the beach. Brown pelicans will typically be plunging in the inlet, and in winter, loons and cormorants fish in the surf. A short nature trail begins from the north end of the beach parking area; it's worth a peek in migration for warblers, vireos, thrushes, and other songbirds.

DIRECTIONS: From I-95, take Okeechobee Road (SR 70) east to US 1. Turn north on US 1 and follow it to North Beach Causeway (SR A1A). Cross the lagoon on the causeway. Follow the signs on the other side to the park, which will be on the right (south) side of the road.

Open 8:00 A.M. to sunset. Best months for birding are October–April.

(772) 468-3985.

www.dep.state.fl.us/parks.

133. Bear Point Sanctuary

DESCRIPTION: Bear Point Sanctuary, managed by St. Lucie County Mosquito Control, includes a series of impoundments lined with mangroves on the Indian River Lagoon. Wading birds are common in the canals and lagoon, and black- and yellow-crowned night herons skulk in the mangroves. The area can have good migratory songbird fallouts during the spring return migration as they make landfall on the coast. Worth a visit if you're in the area—you never know what surprise bird you might find at a site, until you stop and look!

DIRECTIONS: From US 1 in Fort Pierce, go east on Seaway Drive, across the Indian River to south SR A1A. The sanctuary is approximately two miles south on SR A1A, on the right (west) side of the road.

Open twenty-four hours a day. Best months for birding are October–April.

(772) 462-1685.

134. Pinelands

DESCRIPTION: A beautiful property that is a part of the St. Lucie County environmental lands program, Pinelands is located in a remote western part of the county. Watch for turkeys, bobwhite, wood storks, and caracaras on the drive to the property, as well as a flood of wading birds like glossy ibis in wetlands along the roadside. Park at the entrance area and hike the dike trails east and then south in a series of loop trails. Seasonal wetlands are scattered throughout this pine flatwoods property, where you can see sandhill cranes trumpeting in the early morning mist and hear woodpeckers calling each other through the forest. Shorebirds like the margins of these wetlands, as well as the muddy edges of cattle ponds on adjacent pastures, so keep an eye out for a migratory surprise. Follow the directions to the site carefully. It's a beautiful hike, well worth the trip, once you find it!

DIRECTIONS: From Fort Pierce, go west on Okeechobee Road (SR 70) sixteen miles. Turn left (south) just past the cellular tower onto V.P.I. Grove Road (watch for the birding trail sign). Go a mile and a half to the end of the road and turn left (east). Go one mile to the entrance at the end of the road.

Open sunrise to sunset. Best months for birding are October–April.

(772) 462-2525.

www.stlucieco.gov.

135. Savannas Preserve State Park

DESCRIPTION: This vast preserve is one of the foremost ephemeral wetlands in Florida, second only to the Everglades in its status as a freshwater savannah. Originally a saltwater bay, it became freshwater as sea level dropped, and today is rarely more than two to four feet deep at any point. Recharged by rainwater, its levels fluctuate and sustain birds from sandhill cranes to wood storks and migratory ducks. By parking at the corral-fenced gate, you can hike the property through the flatwoods to the savannah overlook at the north end of the trail, or you can choose to tow your canoe in and explore by paddle. Wading birds nest throughout the wetland, so when you see congregations of birds, please respect them and maintain a three-hundred-foot distance from them for their well-being. Other sites in this large property are available for canoeing and hiking access; contact the preserve in advance to make arrangements for your group.

DIRECTIONS: From Fort Pierce, take US 1 south to Walton Road. Travel two miles east on Walton Road to the corral-fenced parking area on the left (north) side of the road.

Open 8:00 A.M. to sunset. Best months for birding are October–April.

(561) 340-7530.

www.dep.state.fl.us/parks.

Resources for Birdwatchers

Organizations

Audubon of Florida

444 Brickell Avenue, Suite 850, Miami, FL 33130; (305) 371-6399; www.audubonofflorida.org or National Audubon Society at www.audubon.org. Membership in the national organization includes membership in state and local chapters.

American Birding Association (ABA)

PO Box 6599, Colorado Springs, CO 80934; (719) 578-9703; www.americanbirding.org. ABA's website offers an online bookstore and helpful links to a wealth of bird-related resources.

Cornell Lab of Ornithology

159 Sapsucker Woods Road, Ithaca, NY 14850; www.birds.cornell.edu. Citizen scientists can participate in Project FeederWatch, Classroom FeederWatch, Birdhouse Network, and more.

Media for Birders

Basic Guides

Guide to the Birds of the Eastern United States, by Roger Tory Peterson, 4th ed. (Houghton Mifflin, 1998).

Field Guide to the Birds of North America, 3d ed. (National Geographic Society, 1999).

Stokes Field Guide to Birds: Eastern Region, by Donald and Lillian Stokes (Little, Brown, 1996).

All the Birds of North America: American Bird Conservancy's Field Guide (Harper Collins Perennial, 1997).

Birds of North America: A Guide to Field Identification, by Chandler S. Robbins,

Bertel Bruun, and Herbert S. Zim (Golden Press, 1983; rev. ed., St. Martin's Press, 2001).

Where to Go

Birder's Guide to Florida, by Bill Pranty, Lane ABA Birdfinding Guide Series no. 175 (American Birding Association, 1996).

Florida Wildlife Viewing Guide, by Susan Cerulean and Ann Morrow (Falcon Press, 1993).

Listen to This

Bird Songs of Florida, by Geoffrey A. Keller (Cornell Lab of Ornithology, 1997; CD).

Field Guide to Bird Songs of Eastern and Central North America, keyed to Peterson's *Field Guide to Birds East of the Rockies* (Houghton Mifflin; CD).

Sounds of Florida's Birds, by John William Hardy (tape; also on www.flmnh. ufl.edu/natsci/ornithology/sounds.htm).

Checklists

Checklists help you in two ways: they enable you to track your sightings, and they reduce the number of birds you have to worry about identifying. Many parks and refuges publish their own site-specific bird lists, available on request.

ABA Checklist, 5th ed. Available through ABA.

Field Checklist of Florida Birds. Available for a nominal fee from Audubon of Florida, 1331 Palmetto Avenue, Suite 110, Winter Park, FL 32789, or download a copy from their website, www.audubonofflorida.org.

Checklist of Florida Birds. To obtain a copy, write to the Wings Over Florida Birdwatching Certificate Program at the Florida Fish and Wildlife Conservation Commission,* or call (850) 414-3831.

Other Publications

Bird Watching Basics. Available from the Florida Fish and Wildlife Conservation Commission.* View it on-line at www.floridabirdingtrail.com/Birdbasics.htm.

Planting a Refuge for Wildlife. What to plant to attract and feed birds; nest box construction and other resources. Available from the Florida Fish and Wildlife Conservation Commission.*

What Have You Done for Wildlife Lately? Available from the Florida Fish and Wildlife Conservation Commission.*

Rare Bird Alert Hotlines

Regularly updated recording of rare and unusual sightings.

Statewide: (941) 242-9338. To sign up for regular e-mails of the statewide Rare Bird Alert (RBA) and other electronic sighting lists, point your browser to www.javaswift.com/floridabirds/.

Miami: (305) 667-7337.

Lower Keys: (305) 294-3438.

South Georgia/North Florida: (912) 244-9190.

How You Can Help Birds

Shade-Grown Coffee

Help preserve tropical forest habitat and bird species diversity by buying coffee labeled "shade-grown." For more information, call or check the websites of these organizations: (1) American Birding Association, PO Box 6599, Colorado Springs, CO 80934; (719) 578-9703; www.americanbirding.org; (2) Rainforest Alliance, 65 Bleecker Street, New York, NY 10012; (212) 677-1900; www.rainforest-alliance.org; (3) Smithsonian Migratory Bird Center, National Zoological Park, Washington, DC 20008; www.natzoo.si.edu/smbc.

Migratory Bird Conservancy

One hundred percent of the donations received by this organization fund the conservation of critical habitat for birds. MBC/NFWF, 1120 Connecticut Avenue NW, Suite 900, Washington, DC 20036; www.conservebirds.org.

Florida State Parks

Ongoing volunteer opportunities are available to help birds at Florida's state parks. Contact a park near you for details.

Great Florida Birding Trail

Donations to the Trail benefit site enhancements for birds and birders. Send your check to the Wildlife Foundation of Florida, PO Box 6181, Tallahassee, FL 32314-6181. In the "for" section of your check, please reference "GFBT."

Especially for Young Birders

A Field Guide to the Birds Coloring Book, by Roger Tory Peterson and Peter Alden (Houghton Mifflin, 1982).

Peterson First Guide to Birds of North America, by Roger Tory Peterson (Houghton Mifflin, 1986).

Sharing the Wonder of Birds with Kids, by Laura Erickson (Pfeifer-Hamilton, 1997).

Birdwise, by Pamela M. Hickman (Addison-Wesley, 1988).

A Bird's-Eye View. ABA's newsletter for young birders. For more information, visit ABA's young birder's website at www.americanbirding.org/ygbgen.htm.

TeenBirdchat is a listserver dedicated to young birders. Subscribe by e-mailing your name, age, and location (with a request to be added to the list) to teenbirdinfo@nbhc.com.

Especially for Teachers

A Guide to Bird Education Resources: Migratory Birds of the Americas, published by Partners in Flight. An abbreviated version of the book is available at their website, www.partnersinflight.org.

Recycle Your Old Binoculars

Donated equipment is used for conservation projects in Latin America and the Caribbean. Visit their website at www.americanbirding.org/consbex.htm.

Did You Know?

You can earn free full-color birding certificates just for documenting the species you have seen in Florida. Certificates are available at four achievement levels. Write to the Wings Over Florida Birdwatching Certificate Program at the Florida Fish and Wildlife Conservation Commission.[1]

Traveler's Tip

The *Florida Atlas & Gazetteer* (DeLorme) features detailed maps based on topographic data. They are indispensable for finding birding sites described in various guides. Available in bookstores or through ABA.

Note

* Florida Fish and Wildlife Conservation Commission (FWC), 620 South Meridian Street, Tallahassee, FL 32399-1600; www.floridaconservation.org. Charges may apply to certain publications.

Index Chart

Site number	Site name	Educational	Good for beginners	Wading birds (large numbers)	Shorebirds in season	Songbird migration	Raptor migration	Limpkin	Painted bunting	Red-cockaded woodpecker	Florida scrub-jay	Roseate spoonbill	Crested caracara	Snail kite	Purple gallinule	Swallow-tailed kite
1	Fort Clinch State Park	•	•		•		•		•							
2	The Nature Center at Amelia Island Plantation	•	•						•							
3	Amelia Island State Park															
4	Big Talbot Island State Park		•		•		•		•							
5	Little Talbot Island State Park	•	•		•	•	•		•							
6	E. Dale Joyner Nature Preserve at Pelotes Island	•	•						•							
7	Cedar Point					•			•							
8	Kingsley Plantation		•			•			•							
9	Fort George Island Cultural State Park		•			•			•							
10	Huguenot Memorial Park				•		•									
11	Fort Caroline National Memorial and Theodore Roosevelt Area	•	•			•			•							
12	Kathryn Abbey Hanna Park		•		•		•									
13	Ralph E. Simmons State Forest															•
14	Jennings State Forest															•
15	Mike Roess Gold Head Branch State Park		•												•	
16	Guana River Wildlife Management Area			•	•	•	•		•			•				•
17	Guana River State Park		•	•	•	•	•		•							•
18	St. Augustine Alligator Farm	•	•	•												
19	Anastasia State Park		•		•	•	•		•							
20	Fort Matanzas National Monument	•	•		•		•		•							
21	Faver-Dykes State Park				•				•							•
22	Princess Place Preserve								•							•
23	Washington Oaks Gardens State Park	•	•			•	•		•		•					

Site number	Site name	Educational	Good for beginners	Wading birds (large numbers)	Shorebirds in season	Songbird migration	Raptor migration	Limpkin	Painted bunting	Red-cockaded woodpecker	Florida scrub-jay	Roseate spoonbill	Crested caracara	Snail kite	Purple gallinule	Swallow-tailed kite
24	Ravine Gardens State Park		•													
25	Caravelle Ranch Wildlife Management Area															•
26	Welaka State Forest	•														•
27	Welaka National Fish Hatchery and Aquarium	•	•	•												•
28	Ocala National Forest: Salt Springs							•		•	•					•
29	Sportsman's Cove		•		•			•								
30	Silver River State Park		•					•								•
31	Ocklawaha Prairie Restoration Area			•	•		•									•
32	Haw Creek Preserve at Russell Landing		•													
33	Bulow Creek State Park		•		•	•										•
34	North Peninsula State Park				•		•				•					
35	Tomoka State Park	•	•		•	•			•							•
36	Ocala National Forest: Alexander Springs	•	•					•		•	•					•
37	Sunnyhill Restoration Area		•	•			•									
38	Emeralda Marsh Conservation Area		•	•			•								•	•
39	Emeralda Marsh Conservation Area (Treasure Island entrance)		•	•			•									•
40	Hidden Waters Preserve															
41	Lake George State Forest		•						•							•
42	DeLeon Springs State Park		•													•
43	Lake Woodruff National Wildlife Refuge	•	•	•	•											•
44	Hontoon Island State Park		•						•							•
45	Blue Spring State Park	•	•													•
46	Lyonia Preserve	•	•								•					

Site number	Site name	Educational	Good for beginners	Wading birds (large numbers)	Shorebirds in season	Songbird migration	Raptor migration	Limpkin	Painted bunting	Red-cockaded woodpecker	Florida scrub-jay	Roseate spoonbill	Crested caracara	Snail kite	Purple gallinule	Swallow-tailed kite
47	Lake Ashby Park															•
48	Smyrna Dunes Park		•		•	•	•		•							
49	Rock Springs Run State Reserve		•								•					•
50	Seminole State Forest										•					•
51	Lower Wekiva River Preserve State Park		•								•					•
52	Wekiwa Springs State Park	•	•													
53	Lake Jesup Wilderness Area															
54	Audubon Center for Birds of Prey	•	•													
55	Mead Gardens					•										
56	Lake Proctor Wilderness Area		•													
57	Geneva Wilderness Area		•													
58	Little Big Econ State Forest: Kilbee Tract			•	•			•				•				•
59	Little Big Econ State Forest: Demetree Tract															•
60	Orlando Wetlands Park			•											•	•
61	Tosohatchee State Reserve		•			•							•			•
62	Merritt Island National Wildlife Refuge	•	•	•	•				•		•	•				
63	Canaveral National Seashore (north entrance)	•	•		•							•				
64	River Breeze Park		•		•							•				
65	Scottsmoor Landing								•							
66	Buck Lake Conservation Area (west entrance)							•								•
67	Buck Lake Conservation Area (east entrance)										•					•
68	Seminole Ranch Conservation Area								•							•
69	Parrish Park–Titusville		•		•											
70	Canaveral National Seashore (south entrance)	•	•		•		•				•	•				
71	Hatbill Park		•	•								•				•

Site number	Site name	Educational	Good for beginners	Wading birds (large numbers)	Shorebirds in season	Songbird migration	Raptor migration	Limpkin	Painted bunting	Red-cockaded woodpecker	Florida scrub-jay	Roseate spoonbill	Crested caracara	Snail kite	Purple gallinule	Swallow-tailed kite
72	Lake Louisa State Park															•
73	Tibet-Butler Preserve	•	•													
74	Gatorland		•	•												
75	The Nature Conservancy's Disney Wilderness Preserve	•	•								•					•
76	Moss Park		•	•												
77	Split Oak Mitigation Park															
78	Lake Lizzie Nature Preserve															
79	Fox Lake Park		•													
80	Blue Heron Wetlands Treatment Facility		•	•	•										•	
81	Kennedy Point Park				•											
82	Pine Island Conservation Area															
83	J. G. Bourbeau Park				•									•		•
84	Kelly Park				•											
85	Port's End Park															
86	Jetty Maritime Park		•		•											
87	Rotary Park at Merritt Island	•														
88	Lori Wilson Park	•	•		•	•	•		•							
89	Tenoroc Fish Management Area	•	•	•												
90	Saddle Creek Park		•			•										
91	Lake Hollingsworth		•	•	•										•	
92	Peace River Park	•														•
93	Lake Region Audubon's Street Nature Center	•	•													
94	Eagle Ridge Mall		•		•											
95	Lake Kissimmee State Park		•	•	•				•		•			•	•	•

Site number	Site name	Educational	Good for beginners	Wading birds (large numbers)	Shorebirds in season	Songbird migration	Raptor migration	Limpkin	Painted bunting	Red-cockaded woodpecker	Florida scrub-jay	Roseate spoonbill	Crested caracara	Snail kite	Purple gallinule
96	Bok Tower Gardens	•	•												
97	Lake Wailes	•	•												
98	Ridge Audubon Nature Center	•	•												
99	Lake Wales Ridge State Forest: Walk-in-the-Water Tract										•				•
100	Lake Wales Ridge State Forest: Arbuckle Tract										•				•
101	Forever Florida	•	•										•		•
102	Joe Overstreet Landing		•					•					•	•	•
103	Three Lakes Wildlife Management Area	•						•		•	•		•	•	•
104	Brevard Zoo	•	•												
105	Rotary Park at Suntree				•										
106	Wickham Park														
107	Lake Washington Park														•
108	Lake Washington: Sarno Road Extension							•					•	•	•
109	Erna Nixon Park		•												
110	Turkey Creek Sanctuary	•	•			•									
111	Malabar Scrub Sanctuary										•				
112	Coconut Point Park				•		•								
113	Honest John's Fish Camp	•	•	•					•			•			
114	T. M. Goodwin Waterfowl Management Area		•	•	•								•		•
115	St. Sebastian River State Buffer Preserve (north entrance)									•	•		•		•
116	St. Sebastian River State Buffer Preserve (south entrance)									•	•		•		•
117	Sebastian Inlet State Park	•	•	•	•		•		•			•			

Site number	Site name	Educational	Good for beginners	Wading birds (large numbers)	Shorebirds in season	Songbird migration	Raptor migration	Limpkin	Painted bunting	Red-cockaded woodpecker	Florida scrub-jay
118	Environmental Learning Center	•	•								
119	Blue Cypress Conservation Area			•		•					
120	Indian River County Wetlands Treatment Facility			•							
121	Oslo Riverfont Conservation Area (ORCA)	•	•	•	•	•		•			
122	Highlands Hammock State Park	•	•				•				•
123	Istokpoga Park		•						•		•
124	Hickory Hammock										
125	Lake June-in-Winter Scrub State Park						•				
126	Prairie Bird Long Loop (starting point)		•						•		
127	Prairie Bird Short Loop (starting point)		•						•		
128	Kissimmee Prairie Preserve State Park	•							•		
129	Lock 7: Jaycee Park		•	•							
130	Okee-Tantie		•								
131	Indrio Savannahs						•				
132	Fort Pierce Inlet State Park			•	•						
133	Bear Point Sanctuary			•	•						
134	Pinelands		•								•
135	Savannas Preserve State Park	•	•	•							•

Contributors

Reed Bowman, assistant research biologist at Archbold Biological Station near Lake Placid, studies the impact of suburbanization on the demography of Florida scrub-jays.

Julie A. Brashears is the Birding Trail coordinator for the Florida Fish and Wildlife Conservation Commission. After training as a biologist at Duke University, she returned to Florida, working to conserve the birds she grew up watching in rural Seminole County.

Susan I. Cerulean writes about conservation from Tallahassee and was the first coordinator of the Florida Fish and Wildlife Conservation Commission's Watchable Wildlife Program.

Jim Cox is a biologist at Tall Timbers Research Station north of Tallahassee. He studies the birds of southeastern pinewoods and teaches birding classes.

Nancy Douglass is a nongame wildlife biologist with the Florida Fish and Wildlife Conservation Commission. She lives, and worries, in Lakeland, with her husband and a small menagerie.

R. Todd Engstrom, a central Florida native who loves the smell of smoke in the piney woods, is a graduate of Florida State University and has been the staff vertebrate ecologist at Tall Timbers Research Station since 1990.

Jeff Gore has been a wildlife biologist with the Florida Fish and Wildlife Conservation Commission in Panama City for fourteen years. He has helped direct several surveys of shorebirds and seabirds throughout Florida.

Paul Gray is manager of Audubon's Ordway-Whittell Kissimmee Prairie Sanctuary in Okeechobee County. His love of wild Florida and persistent advocacy are evident in the conservation successes of the Lake Okeechobee region.

Susan D. Jewell is a biologist for the United States Fish and Wildlife Service in Washington, D.C., and writes about endangered species. She is the author of *Exploring Wild South Florida* and *Exploring Wild Central Florida*.

Ken Meyer, research ecologist and codirector of the Avian Research and Conservation Institute, is widely regarded as the principal authority on swallow-tailed kites in North America.

Joan Morrison, currently assistant professor of conservation biology at Trinity College in Connecticut, focuses her research on birds and conservation issues on private lands.

Ann Morrow is a Tallahassee-based freelance writer who has been writing about the Florida environment in magazines and newspapers for the past fifteen years. She is coauthor, with Susan Cerulean, of *The Florida Wildlife Viewing Guide,* and her essay "A Ribbon of Wilderness" was anthologized in *The Wild Heart of Florida* (University Press of Florida, 1999).

Matthew Mullenix is a falconer and former field biologist for the Florida Fish and Wildlife Conservation Commission. He now lives in Baton Rouge, Louisiana, with his wife and two noisy Harris hawks.

Steve Nesbitt is a biologist with the Florida Fish and Wildlife Conservation Commission and project leader for whooping crane reintroduction in Florida.

Jenny Novak is a regional education specialist in the Florida Fish and Wildlife Conservation Commission's Lakeland office.

Tom Palmer is an award-winning environmental reporter at the *Ledger* in Lakeland. He is a native Floridian who watches birds, butterflies, and everything else interesting in the natural world.

Joanna Taylor is a refuge ranger with Pelican Island National Wildlife Refuge, managing interpretive programs and the volunteer program. She has worked at Merritt Island National Wildlife Refuge, as well as for the United States Fish and Wildlife Service on whooping crane and other avian captive propagation programs.

Noel Wamer, a Florida native, has worked as a biologist in environmental and transportation consulting. He has been an active birder for more than thirty years.

Glen Woolfenden, distinguished research professor at the University of South Florida and research associate at Archbold Biological Station, has been conducting an intensive study of the ecology and behavior of a population of Florida scrub-jays in native habitat at Archbold since 1969.